THE
PSYCHIC POWER
OF ANIMALS

THE
PSYCHIC POWER
OF ANIMALS

HOW TO COMMUNICATE
WITH YOUR PET

CASSANDRA EASON

PIATKUS

First published in 2003 by
Judy Piatkus (Publishers) Limited
5 Windmill Street
London W1T 2JA
e-mail: info@piatkus.co.uk

*A catalogue record for this book is available
from the British Library*

ISBN 0 7499 2451 9

Edited by Jan Cutler
Text design by Zena Flax

This book has been printed on paper manufactured
with respect for the environment using wood from
managed sustainable resources

Data manipulation by Phoenix Photosetting, Chatham, Kent
Printed and bound in Great Britain by
Antony Rowe Ltd, Chippenham, Wiltshire

Contents

Introduction:
The intuitive
link of love

PEOPLE WHO ARE ANIMAL lovers are invariably kind and trust-worthy, and are receptive to their own instincts and intuition. Because of this, they form strong links with their pets that go beyond ordinary levels of communication. This same intuitive awareness also enables them to communicate with wild birds and wildlife in the garden, woodland and sanctuary, as well as butterflies and more exotic creatures.

Because the creatures themselves are very special, the intuitive process is reciprocated. For thousands of years pets have given unconditional love, trust and protection to their owners. They have endowed those who care for them with insights, providing a simple but wise and deeply spiritual per-spective on the world, which for many people has become obscured by the pressures of twenty-first-century living.

THE PSYCHIC WORLD OF ANIMALS AND BIRDS

I have investigated the psychic and intuitive powers of humans throughout the world in depth for over 15 years, and have discovered that many ordinary people possess an evolved sixth sense that has alerted them to danger or enabled them to communicate wordlessly to another human, even perhaps across miles. During the course of my research I have learned that the deep instinctive bond between animal and human is no less evolved. A significant number of pet owners can recall at least one instance when their animal or bird has apparently read their thoughts or alerted them to an unreliable stranger or potential hazard, to which they had been previously unaware. This deep unconscious link is based on the enhanced instincts possessed by animals, combined with the deep love felt by pet owners that enables them to understand and communicate with their pets and other creatures in ways not measurable or accountable by current scientific knowledge.

ABOUT THIS BOOK

Throughout the book I have described numerous examples of these significant bonds between humans and the animal kingdom – sometimes the stories are quite amazing. As a pet owner and pet lover for more than 50 years, I have enjoyed many insights into the secret world of pets and the indigenous wildlife I have watched outside the window. When I studied psychology, I realised that animal behaviour was so complex that we are left with more questions than logical answers. However, I also discovered that there is a significant amount of knowledge based on patterns drawn from the everyday world.

This ability to communicate, which has now been thoroughly researched by the Cambridge biochemist Dr Rupert Sheldrake (see page 19) and others, can allow us to strengthen the unspoken channels of communication and to understand our pets as spiritual beings with much to teach us, providing we acknowledge it. With this in mind, in the following chapters I have suggested ways that you can develop deeper communication with the animals and birds with which you share your life and immediate environment as well as understanding how deeper rhythms in the natural world can affect the most city-sophisticated pooch or cat. This is possible because, deep down, domesticated as well as wild creatures are still connected with nature. What might seem like sudden, inexplicable and quirky behaviour from our pet is unlikely to indicate the need for a visit to a pet psychologist, but instead the creature perhaps just needs to be allowed to roll in the autumn leaves or to build a den behind the sofa against the winter chills outside the door.

I have also described ways to heal your pets. These are not intended as substitutes for veterinary expertise but to supplement conventional care and to reduce the stress in a creature's life that can make them more susceptible to illness or accidental injury. We can also benefit from the healing power of animals: we can consciously as well as unconsciously learn to draw the healing strength and comfort we need in sad or lonely moments from the unwavering affection and loyalty of household animals.

Finally, I do believe that animals have a soul and seem to survive death just as humans do and that they retain memory of and affection for their former owners; this has been confirmed to me by evidence from countless sources. The grief on losing a beloved pet is so acute it may last for years. I have, therefore, suggested ways we can revive the love of a beloved pet, even if not its physical presence; this will help to heal grief so that we can learn to love another creature that can bring future happiness and companionship.

PETS IN HISTORY

Our pets originally came from wild animals. Perhaps these were individuals of the species that came close to settlements and were naturally responsive to people. Indeed, the findings of three research teams, reported in November 2002 in the UK *Science* magazine, suggested that 95 per cent of all dogs have evolved from three founding female wolves, tamed by humans living in or near China less than 15,000 years ago. Even dogs in the New World have their origins in Eastern Asia. According to Carles Vila, of Uppsala University, Sweden, one of the team studying the New World dogs, they travelled via Europe and Scandinavia with the colonists. Dogs became invaluable as hunting animals, and because they also protected vulnerable humans, the mutual dependence between dogs and humans was created, and we can see it today in even the most pampered urban pooch.

The ancient Egyptians were devoted to cats in preference to dogs and the wealthy would accord their pet cats elaborate burials, often in the tomb of a family member. The tomb walls would be decorated with painted dishes of milk and food as well as magical formulas so that the pets would be fed in the afterlife. So important were cats to the ancient Egyptians that if there was a fire, the cats were rescued with the humans.

The first authenticated accounts of cats as human companions date from about 2000 BCE when it appears that the kittens of the African wild cat or smaller swamp cat were adopted, and gradually, over generations, became domesticated. Originally the cats were used to protect the all-valuable grain stores and domestic larders from rats and mice, but over time love grew.

Egyptian tomb paintings also show cats, rather than dogs, retrieving game birds. They acted like modern-day hunting dogs, retrieving the birds that their owners had killed with spears.

The birds were hunted in nets and with spears in the papyrus marshes surrounding the major cities. Cats were also sacred to the cat goddess, Bast (or Bastet), who was shown in human form with a cat's head. Archaeologists have excavated vast acres of cat cemeteries at Bubastis, Bast's cult centre on the Nile Delta, where it is estimated that there are four million mummified cats buried, (many cats were kept in the temples for sacrifices). As well as Bubastis, there were huge cat cemeteries at Giza and Abydos, and Dendera in Upper Egypt.

FROM THE ASHES OF THE WORLD TRADE CENTER

Pets can demonstrate amazing altruism and self-sacrifice towards other humans apart from their owners, which may go far beyond their own survival instincts. For me the most dramatic and uplifting stories of animal devotion come from the aftermath of the World Trade Center disaster on 11 September 2001. There were many heroic rescue dogs that assisted hour after hour in choking conditions in their attempts to save survivors. But the most remarkable story was that of Dorado, the guide dog that was at work as usual that day with his blind owner, Omar Eduardo Rivera, a computer technician. Omar became trapped on the 71st floor of the World Trade Center, North Tower, when the first hijacked airliner crashed into the building. Fearing there was no way he could escape, Omar unleashed Dorado, patted him and told him to go. But the four-year-old Labrador retriever refused to leave his master in spite of the heat, flying glass and panicking crowds who were rushing past. At one point Dorado was actually carried away by the rush of people but fought against the tide and returned to guide his owner down 70 flights of stairs and out into the street.

Another heroic Trade Center animal was a mother cat who cared for her three kittens for two weeks when they became buried in the basement of a restaurant destroyed by the blast. She created a nest for them in a carton of table napkins. When she was rescued she was dehydrated and weighed less than half her normal body weight, but the kittens were fine. The cat was called Hope and the kittens, Freedom, Amber and Flag.

THE ALTRUISM OF ANIMALS

Both Dorado and Hope acted in ways that would be described as heroic if they were humans, and I could fill a whole book with similar accounts of animals that have saved the lives of owners, strangers or their own young. For a number of years now I have been collecting case studies from personal knowledge and news reports and have hundreds of similar authenticated cases.

If you enter 'heroic pets' or 'brave animals' on your Web browser you will be able to read accounts from around the world of animals – not only dogs, but also horses and even parrots – that have alerted their owners to danger or rescued them from dangerous situations. Such cases go back through history. One of the lesser-known heroes of the *Titanic* was Rigel, a huge, black Newfoundland dog, that was owned by First Officer Murdoch and that saved the lives of the passengers and crew in Lifeboat Four. In the darkness, the lifeboat was drifting out of control into the path of the rescue steamer, SS *Carpathia*, and in danger of being crushed. Those in the lifeboat were too exhausted to call out when they heard the *Carpathia* approaching. Rigel had been swimming in front of the lifeboat for three hours in the icy water. When he saw the *Carpathia* he began to swim between it and the lifeboat barking until the crew of the *Carpathia* heard him; he guided the lifeboat to safety so that the passengers could be transferred to the rescue steamer. However, Rigel refused to rest even then, but stayed on the lifeboat deck with his front paws against the deck rail, looking for his master who had drowned.

What can we learn from such accounts? That if we open our hearts to our pets we will be rewarded ten times over, maybe not in life-and-death situations but by their ongoing love and loyalty which will be demonstrated in countless small ways. We will receive the same response if we show our affection to animals that have been abandoned or neglected.

Much of what I have described is already present in your relationship with animals and birds, and sometimes it is merely a matter of becoming aware of these almost magical links for them to emerge spontaneously. So there is no complex course to follow, only pointers, suggestions and psychic games you can play with your pet that you will find pleasurable and will often confirm what you already know – that your animal was the right choice for you and is truly special.

THE INTELLIGENCE OF ANIMALS

We talk about dumb animals, but a pet will not only go against its natural instinct to flee danger but may also resort to ingenious methods to warn its owner of danger. Take the example of Roc, a cross-retriever that was owned by Roosevelt and Linda who live in New Bern, North Carolina. On 25 June 1996, in the middle of the night, lightning struck the attic of their home and started a fire. Roc barked but was unable to wake his owners or their teenage children. At last he rang the doorbell continuously until they woke. Everyone escaped, although the family lost all their possessions. Roosevelt told reporters that prior to the fire Roc had not been trained to ring the doorbell.

Dogs are the most intelligent of all creatures. Indeed in a study carried out in 2002 by researchers at Harvard University and the Wolf Hollow Wolf Sanctuary in America, findings indicated that young puppies of nine weeks old were better at interpreting social cues from humans than adult chimpanzees, who are among our closest animal relations. Brian Hare, who carried out the Harvard experiments, confirmed that puppies were as skilled as older dogs and said this indicated that the ability was innate and not learned.

The work carried out by assistance dogs throughout the world for disabled human owners is perhaps the strongest example of this intelligence. However, I discovered when I talked to Alan, who lives near Petersfield in Hampshire, that this amazing intelligence is only part of the gift an assistance animal makes in transforming its owner's life. Indeed Alan is convinced that the amazing powers of the dogs come not only from training but also from pure love of the animal for its owner (see also the story of Gareth and his dog, Hero, on pages 92–4 and for details of the Canine Partners for Independence training centre in Resources). Canine Partners for Independence is an organisation that trains dogs to assist disabled owners in a wide range of tasks, from helping their owner to get dressed to operating a washing machine, as well as ensuring their safety.

Alan is a former Navy weapons engineer, who suffered a serious head injury during the Gulf War and is now in a wheelchair. Endal, Alan's dog partner from Canine Partners for Independence, helped to restore Alan's confidence and has, according to Alan, given him back his life:

> I was brought home virtually dead from the Gulf War and before Endal came to live with me I was heading for a War Pension Home ... I did not speak and suffered memory loss.
>
> I was taken to the Canine Partners for Independence training centre where I would sit in my wheelchair, hidden in a quiet corner of the training centre in a world of my own, never wanting to communicate with anyone except the dogs. Endal was a failed Canine Partners dog; he was sitting at the other end of the training centre – another misfit not prepared to work for the trainers and unwilling to do even the simplest tasks without a great deal of prompting. He was a problem dog that was causing a headache for everyone involved.

But together Alan and Endal, the two misfits, became an unstoppable team, and they now work towards helping others with disabilities. How does Alan explain this apparent miracle?

> My guardian angel has four legs not two. Endal gave me back the key to my life and lit up my mind. When Endal came up to my wheelchair we intuitively found each other. Endal had not done any intensive training, the only training he had was while being puppy-walked (basic obedience) so everything had to be learned on our own. Despite this, Endal always seemed to know what it was that I wanted, even before I was aware of it, he just read me like a book.
>
> I really can't recall most of my past because of my head injury, but Endal has given me so much of a future to look forward to that nothing else really matters. I feel my life was like a puzzle thrown into the wind. But Endal has bought back the pieces day by day. Yes, there will always be large parts missing but Endal is making sense of what remains. He has saved my life, my marriage and

my relationship with my children, and he has taught me to love again.

Of course it took almost superhuman effort on both Alan and Endal's part to reach that stage, but now the partnership is one that is so close it is seamless, beyond words. Indeed, the PDSA (People's Dispensary for Sick Animals) awarded a gold medal for gallantry to Endal in November 2002 after he helped Alan when he had an accident in a hotel car park. Alan's wheelchair had tipped over and he was trapped; Endal managed to drag his owner free then covered him with the blanket from the wheelchair and moved Alan's mobile phone where he could reach it. Only when Alan regained consciousness did Endal leave him to fetch help.

Endal performs countless tasks for Alan, which enable him to live independently. Most spectacular is Endal's ability to use a cash point machine, which Alan discovered quite by chance.

It was a sunny day and I positioned myself so I could shade the screen of the cash point machine to read it, this meant having to move to get the card, receipt and money. Without being prompted, Endal jumped up and took each item and passed it to me. The people in the queue behind me just clapped and asked, 'How do you teach a dog to do that?' They were as amazed as I was when I said he had never been trained to do it.

Next time we visited the cash point machine I thought, I'll see how clever he is, so I passed him my card with the arrow sticking out of his mouth, and yes, he just jumped up and put it in to the slot first go.'

But, as Alan pointed out, although Endal is now one of the most famous dogs in the UK, 'For me it is not just the amazing things he can do that is so marvellous, it is the way Endal can empathise, whether I am in a high or low mood.'

I suffer from word blindness, where I forget words, but Endal intuitively knows what I want and brings it to me. When we are out, Endal helps with the hidden disability of my memory problems. If I go to cross a road without looking and it is not safe to cross he will keep me waiting. (I cannot calculate distance accurately, and I can think a car is far away enough for it to be safe to cross when in fact it is not!)

We've been there for each other, helping the other on the bad days and sharing in the good days. I can put my hand down by my side day or night and he is always there (this very second he is resting with his head on my feet).

But Alan says he believes all pets are valuable and vital to human happiness, not only wonder dogs like Endal. Whether a dog, cat or budgie, a pet brings unconditional love and understanding.

Most of us see much more subtle examples of our pets' very special nature, but over the weeks and months you and your pet really do become a psychic team. In the next chapter I list 20 ways that indicate the presence of this intuitive bond, not only with pets but also with local wildlife. A number of the methods you may already recognise and the others can easily be developed with any animal or bird, using the bond of affection and some of the suggestions in the following chapters.

THE
PSYCHIC POWER
OF ANIMALS

1 | Your psychic link with animals

W E ALL HAVE INTUITIVE LINKS with our pets and other creatures that occur so commonly that they may not seem special to us. Yet the psychic links that exist spontaneously between pet and owner are the powers that most trained psychics struggle for years to acquire.

20 WAYS TO MEASURE YOUR PSYCHIC LINK WITH ANIMALS

Read through the following and tick any that apply to you:

1 Your love of animals began when you were a small child and you had a whole range of teddy bears and toy animals that you cared for, not to mention injured butterflies, insects and frogs that you kept in your bedroom, to everyone's horror.

2 Sick, lost or injured animals and birds still seem to find their way to your door or, when you are out for a walk, drop at your feet.

3 When you are contemplating going out for the evening or away on a trip, your pet appears inseparable from you even before you begin preparations.

4 Family members report that your pet starts waiting in the hall five or ten minutes before you return from work or a shopping trip, even if you are unexpectedly early or delayed; you may also notice this when other family members are absent.

5 Other people's pets become instant friends even if you have only just met.

6 A pet that is normally boisterous or independent sits quietly close to you if you are ill or unhappy.

7 Your animal growls or hisses at a stranger or new acquaintance who subsequently proves unreliable.

8 Your animal has warned you away from a potential hazard in the dark or in an unknown place by barking, howling or tugging at the leash.

9 When you speak to a strange animal or bird it becomes still and silent rather than moving away or becoming over-excited.

10 You can calm animals or birds by the power of your voice.

11 You can soothe a sick or frightened animal by stroking it.

12 Wild birds or animals come close when you are sitting quietly in the garden, the park or the countryside.

13 You have occasionally seen coloured lights or flashes around your pet or birds in flight.

14 You become deeply distressed by the sight of a badly caged animal or a programme about ill-treated creatures.

15 Your pet becomes upset or restless when you are planning a routine visit to the vet several hours before you get out the pet carrier or mention the visit to a family member.

16 If a pet goes missing you can sometimes instinctively sense where he or she might be, if you concentrate.

17 When you are abroad you feed all the starving cats, pay huge amounts of local currency so that the horses or donkeys pulling carts can have a rest, and vow to join an international animal charity the minute you get home.

18 You know when an elderly or sick animal or bird is ready to let go of life and feel able to stop all treatment except that necessary to keep the pet comfortable.

19 You have known in your heart when an animal has died, whether when lost or having an operation at the vet's or when you have been away from home and left the animal with family or friends.

20 You have sensed, heard, felt or seen a fleeting glimpse of a pet who has died.

If you scored more than eight you have an existing psychic link with your pet and other animals that you can strengthen even more as you try some of the ideas I suggest in this book. If you scored less, you may not as yet have had the opportunity to develop these innate abilities. Alternatively, your animal might need some help to awaken the psychic bond he or she demonstrates in other ways (look at the amazing link that grew between Alan and Endal from unpromising beginnings on pages xiii–xvi). Remember, rescue centre animals may need time to allow trust to grow with a new owner.

You can try the questions again after you have read the book and practised some of the exercises. You will find these intuitive powers increase the more they are used, rather like any ability.

In the next chapter I will describe how you can use your intuition to find the right pet for you, or to understand what made you pick the ugliest mutt at the rescue centre.

2 | Choosing a pet

A S YOU FIGHT FOR a place on the sofa you may be asking yourself, 'How did I end up with this mutt/moggy/half-bald
rabbit?' You remember when you decided to buy a pet: you
had set off for the pedigree cattery or to buy your show dog
with a list of registered names several metres long. You got
lost en route, passed a rescue centre and decided on impulse
just to pop in for a minute. Then you saw *him*: scruffy, with
only half a coat of tangled fur and a life story to melt the
hardest heart. He wagged what passed for a tail and your
heart was lost. Now, well fed and glossy, he is taking up more
than his fair share of houseroom. The problem was that you
had already reserved your prize pet as soon as those liquid
eyes met yours. You phoned the pedigree dealer to say you
would be late. Bad news, the prize-winning pedigree had been
sold by mistake, and you could swear your new friend
smirked as he stepped triumphantly into the back of the car
and into your heart.

This cosmic management can occur even if you already
have pets and perhaps are only half-considering a new addition. On one occasion I had visited the local RSPCA rescue
centre to make a donation and had fallen in love with a beautiful fluffy grey kitten called Archie. I already had four cats;
Archie was tiny and cuddly and would fit in unobtrusively

with the other dominant females. The day came for me to collect Archie, and my five children, then aged from three to 13, piled into the car. When we reached the RSPCA rescue centre we were early and so went for a walk through the cattery. The hugest, most ugly black and white neutered tom, called Simba, sprang into action as we entered, swinging from the bars in his pen, yowling as though singing an operetta, leaping around, performing most unfeline-like tricks and fixing us with the deepest though most unmatching eyes I had ever seen. The children were entranced. But Archie was already booked.

At reception, the animal worker had bad news. Archie had a virus and so could not be released. Would we like to choose another cat? So we chose Simba. On the way home he performed one more trick, using his double-jointed paw to undo the hook on the cat box in the car, to the delight of the children. Thereafter he moved only to eat and, once a year, on my son Jack's birthday, he would bring in a mouse, although his activities as a hunter were non-existent the rest of the year.

Simba's biggest claim to fame was when I was recording a radio broadcast on the phone in the living room for a local radio station. I was taking part in a phone-in on ghosts when a bird fell down the chimney and began to flutter around the room a little dirty but otherwise unharmed. The normally inert Simba decided to give chase and, being ungainly, was knocking ornaments over and papers were flying everywhere while the bird set up a squawk straight from the gates of hell.

At last I managed to push Simba out through the cat flap while a record was played on the radio station, and I spent the rest of the broadcast lying flat on the floor trying to hold the flap down, as Simba, sensing an occasion, pushed against it with his paws, meowing loudly. The broadcast ended, Simba looked at the bird with a distinct lack of enthusiasm and I managed to bundle the bird into a box. It proved no worse for wear and flew off, shaking its feathers contemptuously at the amazed Simba. Although you may think we were tricked into having this crazy animal, Simba has actually been a wonderful addition to our collection of creatures because he was so incredibly loving and gentle and also so docile, he would even travel on the back seat of the car and sit peacefully on my lap while we waited at the vet's.

MAKING A WISE CHOICE

Sometimes the reasons for choosing a particular animal are less obvious and it is only weeks or months later that we realise we could have picked no other creature. Sharon, who lives in Norwich, chose the least beautiful animal for her new pet when she visited the animal rescue centre. But her instinctive choice proved a lifesaver. She told me:

> I really wanted a golden retriever puppy. But they were so expensive we decided to look in a rescue centre. I was attracted to Digby because I felt so sorry for him. He came up to me straight away carrying his big plastic ball to play with. He was such a mess, with hardly any fur on his lower back and a bald patch on his tail. But, as Digby padded towards me, I just knew he was the one.
>
> In August 2001 I brought Digby home. Just three months later he had a full healthy coat of golden fur. The only thing he didn't do was bark or growl. He was just too soft. 'You're no guard dog,' I teased him. How wrong I was.
>
> On 25 January 2002 I left the house at about 8.30 p.m. with Digby to visit my sister. It was dark, but as I walked along the tree-lined path to the green, I felt totally safe. After letting Digby have a run around I shouted to him to come back.
>
> But just as I was pulling his lead out of my pocket, I was grabbed around the neck from behind. I tried to scream for help but I could hardly breathe. The man pulled me down a dirt track into a wooded area and threw me to the ground. I spotted another man waiting in the shadows. The first man knelt on me and dug his knee into my left arm, 'Give me your money,' he snarled.

'I haven't got any,' I kept repeating hysterically.

The other guy started to come towards me. I kicked out as hard as I could and caught him on the shins, screaming at them both to leave me alone. He yanked off my gold bracelet while the other one went for my necklace. In the struggle he ripped open my blouse.

The man standing up urged his accomplice to remove my bra. Sheer panic gripped me as I realised what they wanted. I struggled to break free. But couldn't move under my attacker's weight. Suddenly I heard a ferocious barking and screams of agony. It was Digby, swinging from the other man's arm and growling as the man tried to shake him off, Digby's jaws clamped on to his flesh.

As the man on top of me finally let me go to help his friend I grabbed my chance. I scrambled to my feet and ran as fast as I could towards the green with Digby at my heels. Shaking violently I dialled 999 on my mobile, hardly able to get the words out, because I was sobbing so hard.

My coat and trousers were covered with mud, my shoes were missing and my blouse was ripped to pieces. At home that night I couldn't stop crying and hugging Digby. Now I always feel safer when Digby is by my side. I never imagined that my gentle dog could be such a hero.

(My thanks to *Best* magazine for allowing me to use this story.)

Sharon felt that she was meant to have Digby, and that his actions were his way of showing his gratitude. He had overcome his natural timidity and fears to protect his beloved owner.

ESTABLISHING THE CONNECTION

There can be other ways that can indicate a particular animal is intended to live with us. One very common sign is when a young animal shares the birthday of a former pet or was born on the day or the anniversary when a beloved animal companion died. Some owners feel instinctively that the new pet has been guided to him or her, not as a replacement for the lost animal, as each animal is unique, but as consolation and as a way of overcoming grief.

Bev runs Home Rescue, an animal organisation that helps to find abandoned animals a new home in the north of England. She told me how she lost her beloved cat, Amber, suddenly and unexpectedly on 7 June 2001:

> Some months after Amber's death, we decided to buy a deerhound after we had visited Crufts Dog Show in March 2001. The breeding bitch we chose was three weeks' pregnant at the time. The puppies were born on 6 April 2002, but the breeder told us she would not let them go for ten weeks. There were only three pups and she assigned us Darcy, the runt of the litter, which we did not mind. It was agreed we could collect him on 15 June, close to the anniversary of Amber's death.
>
> On 7 June at 12.45 p.m., the precise time Amber died, I was sitting thinking of Amber when the breeder phoned to say our pup was being bullied by the others and could we collect Darcy as soon as possible. We brought Darcy home the same day – a gift from Amber.

The coincidence of time as well as date confirmed for Bev and her husband that the decision to have Darcy was the right one. Purely on a rational level they were especially receptive to Darcy because of the time and date match, but Bev is convinced the link was more than mere random chance. Indeed, Bev said that this was not the first time she had experienced synchronicity, which the psychotherapist Carl Gustav Jung described as 'meaningful coincidence'.

Bev described another psychic link that occurred after the death of Tess, her beloved dog, which suggested that the deceased animal was somehow giving her blessing to a new animal entering Bev's household:

Our old dog, Tess, had to be put to sleep on 15 July 1998. A few months later, we agreed to adopt a Main Coone cat. We went to collect her, without knowing much about her (she'd come to my attention via a friend who ran a cat rescue centre). When the owner handed me the cat and her pedigree papers, it turned out that she had been born on the day Tess died.

How can this connection work?

Modern science is becoming increasingly aware that everything is made up of connected particles of constantly moving energy. Some researchers believe that humans and animals emit particular frequencies of energies, and in Chapter 5 I will describe how these unique energy patterns function and interact with the energy systems of other people and animals. These individual energy fields are more compatible with some people and animals than with others. This would explain how particular animals seem to tune in with us emotionally, and how animals and humans are drawn together by what seems to be pure coincidence but is actually a kind of intuitive radar. That this is a meaningful coincidence is shown by the fact that the match invariably proves successful over the months and years.

Of course this is just one theory, but there certainly seems to be an intangible chemistry between humans and animals that brings together particular pets and their owners in sometimes the most unlikely ways.

Using a pendulum

When you choose a pet you will probably want to leave any decision-making until you arrive at a cattery, rescue centre or breeder's so that you can see which animal you strike up an instant rapport with. However, you can use a pendulum to guide you to the best location to find your pet. This method will work whether you are looking for a horse, a parrot or a rabbit as well as for dogs and cats.

Pendulums are one of the few psychic methods trusted by science and industry and have had spectacular success in finding water and oil for many years. Latterly, they have also been used in war situations for locating enemy submarines and landmines, sometimes using only a map (see my book *Pendulum Dowsing*, Piatkus 2000).

A pendulum is simply a weight on a chain. It can be made from crystal, metal or wood or can even be a favourite pendant, and is useful for all forms of decision-making. A pendulum operates by psychokinesis: your hand is guided by your unconscious mind to move the pendulum towards the correct choice from a selection of possibilities listed on a piece of paper.

We rarely recognise or trust the automatic radar that operates in our unconscious mind. But when we use the pendulum it gives us an external and tangible expression of our automatic radar. My own research has shown that it is for this reason that the pendulum method works time and time again.

Deep down in our intuition we have all kinds of buried useful information, and pets are remarkably efficient at loosening our intuitive inhibitions. A pendulum held over a written list of possible locations will reflect our hidden psychic awareness of where we will find our new pet (see also pages 30–1 How to find a lost animal or bird). The pendulum responds by a tugging, downward movement or a sudden heaviness over one choice on the list. Simply follow the steps below:

1 Research the places where you might be able to locate your pet; for example, your local paper, through friends or colleagues, a rescue centre, a registered breeder and so on. On paper draw either a circle and divide it up into segments or make a grid of squares, according to the number of possible locations or options you have found.

2 Label each segment with a single option of where your pet might be found.

3 Allow any previously unconsidered ideas to emerge quite naturally when you have exhausted your list, by sitting quietly holding the pendulum freely over the paper and allowing your mind to go blank.

4 Pass the pendulum slowly over each option in turn, 2–3 centimetres (¾–1¼ inches) above the writing. You will feel it pull down as though dragged by gravity over one particular option. Although this option might seem the least likely it will usually be justified by subsequent events.

DREAMING ABOUT ANIMALS

Sometimes we may receive a signal that a particular animal is intended for us through a dream. This is not in any way weird or spooky. Rather it is the radar in our unconscious mind alerting us that a specific kind of animal or even one individual creature is right for us even if our conscious choice would be different. There is no doubt that the unconscious part of ourselves possesses information that we cannot access while we are awake or consciously focusing on an issue. Pet owners tend to be especially alert to this form of guidance because they are sensitive to their own intuitive processes and therefore tuned in to the needs of animals, even those they may not yet have met.

Pamela from Eastbourne described to me a dream that she had at a time when she was not even considering getting a pet.

I had a dream that I owned a black, tailless Manx cat, though I didn't have a cat at all at the time. But after I had the dream I decided I would quite like a cat. Later that week a friend at work mentioned in conversation that her husband's friend had to find a new home for his cat as he was going abroad. So I offered to go along and see if I liked it. The cat was black as in my dream but it wasn't a Manx. However, it didn't have a tail because it had been involved in a car accident and lost it. Needless to say I took it home.

Pamela's dream alerted her to a subconscious desire to own a cat, and the dream about the tail narrowed down the field so that she was able to recognise *her cat*. Sometimes our conscious minds can create all kinds of practical obstacles, but the unconscious mind will guide us effortlessly to make the right decisions, if allowed to do so.

USING DREAMS

The psychoanalyst Sigmund Freud called dreams 'the royal road to the unconscious', and Jung, for a while a pupil of Freud, stated that in our dreams we could access material from a collective pool of wisdom that was not limited by time or space. Whether or not you believe dreams can be psychic or are messages from our own personal unconscious depths, they can certainly alert us to unconsidered possibilities and options, as in the case of Pamela above. Many dreams are spontaneous, but you can structure them so that they will focus on a particular issue, in this case choosing a suitable pet.

Both the ancient Egyptians and the Greeks used a technique called 'dream incubation' or 'dreaming true' in which the seeker focused on a particular issue just before sleep in order to obtain an answer while the mind was at its most open to the more psychic sources of wisdom. The following steps give a simple way to do this:

1 Keep a pen and paper by your bed so that you can record details about your dream as soon as you wake up.

2 Before bed, look at an illustrated animal book with a variety of different kinds of pets, even those you are not consciously considering. Spend longer studying the images of any that seem to attract you particularly.

3 Set the book open at your favourite picture, focusing just before sleep on the image rather than the words, because dreams work mainly through symbols.

4 Close your eyes and hold this final image in your mind

as though viewing it on an internal television screen, so it is the last thing you recall before falling asleep.

5 You may then dream of animals, and might even focus on a particular one. If this is a lion, for example, this would suggest you are looking for a courageous pet, even if your choice would be a tiny Jack Russell. You may dream of a distinctively marked pet or an animal you would not have thought about buying, but which gives you great pleasure in the dream.

6 When you wake up, close your eyes and allow the images to flow once more through your mind. Draw any symbols, write notes or scribble down any unusual features of your dream animal before they fade. This happens very quickly after waking, as our mind quickly tidies up the dream experience. If you do not dream of an animal, note any other distinctive dream symbols; these could be location pointers, such as a bank of brilliantly coloured flowers or a clock tower that you may recognise as being in a particular place; for example, close to a pet centre.

You may need to study the same picture just before sleep for several days if you have a very busy life and a lot on your conscious mind. After about a week you may come across the dream animal. If you did not see one in your dream you may find that you recognise the flowers growing in the front garden of the house from which you are going to collect the pet or you might see a similar tower to the dream one near to a rescue centre you have driven past because there was a traffic diversion.

USING VISUALISATION

If you do not have significant dreams, it may be that your subconscious works in a different way. You may be content just to let life lead you to the animal. However, you may

wish to establish in advance a psychic and emotional connection between you and your future pet so that mutual
recognition is instantaneous. In this case you could try visualisation, an effective psychological method of focusing on
what you want.

The power of the mind is greater than we often realise,
and we can make a telepathic connection with an animal that
is on our emotional wavelength through visualisation. We can
create a space in our mind in which we can visualise or imagine our future pet. This works because animals that are
seeking owners are so open that they transmit intuitive vibes
of love into the cosmos and our own radar picks these up
unconsciously.

Even if you find it hard to accept the idea of innate psychic powers, by allowing your mind to form the picture of the
pet, you can open your conscious mind to alternatives that
might actually suit you better than the choice made by your
conscious mind. If you find an entirely different creature
appearing in your visualisation or daydreams it may be a way
of alerting you to an affinity you have with a particular animal
that you had not recognised.

What is more, some people believe that you can draw
the right animal closer to you through an innate psychic
power called psychokinesis – the same power that lies
behind pendulum work. This is the ability of the mind to
draw compatible people, or animals and people, together.
You may have already experienced this in daily life; for
example, you suddenly think of someone you have not met
for years and within an hour you meet him or her in an
unusual place or you receive a totally unexpected phone call
from the person who had also suddenly just thought of
you.

If you have not used a visualisation technique before, it is
often easiest to work after dark and use a large mirror propped
up on a table. This is also a good method to use if you cannot
decide between a particular breed of animal, although you
might have considered the advantages and disadvantages
quite logically.

1 In front of the mirror, light three or four small, squat pink candles or night lights in pink holders. (Pink is a colour associated with affection and loyalty; in time you may see it in the psychic energy field of animals that have lived with humans for a number of years.)

2 Sit behind the candles and imagine a path right in the centre back of the mirror. Imagine an animal or bird whose outline is blurred walking or hopping along it.

3 Relax your eyes so they are half-closed and let your mind build up features and fur or feathers that become clearer as the animal approaches.

4 When the animal is near, close your eyes and then open them and blink. In that moment you may gain a very detailed impression of a creature that may not be at all what you expected but which feels right.

5 Blow out the candles, one by one, requesting in your mind that the animal will find its way into your life, if it is right to be. (Remember, never leave a burning candle unattended.)

Now get on with life and let all the ingredients blend together in the cosmic melting pot.

FINDING YOUR ANIMAL

Within a day or so of a spontaneous or directed intuitive experience you may learn about an animal looking for a home. It may be through a friend of a friend or a work colleague or you may be drawn to an advertisement in a local free sheet that you do not usually read.

If not, visit your local rescue centre where there are young animals as well as older ones. You might find that a particular animal approaches you and that you recognise him or her instantly from your thought work. Alternatively, you may see a particular animal at the back of one of the pens that you recognise from your dream or visualisation; perhaps it is weaker or excluded by the others, but it is watching you.

If you cannot see the animal and no others appeal to you (we all have more than one creature with whom we resonate), ask if there are any animals in the nursery or any that are sick, and you might find *your* pet there. Even if there is a sign saying that no animals are available, ask anyway; if you feel instinctively the time and place are right an animal may just have arrived or a sick one may just be ready to leave quarantine during your visit.

This happened to Linda from Redhill in Surrey. She told me:

> Our new puppy comes from Battersea Dogs Home and we strongly feel she was picked for us. However, on the day we visited the Home, there were signs saying 'No puppies' and 'No family dogs'. When our lengthy interview was over, the rehoming officer went off to find the one pup that might be available that day. Back she came, ages later, and put a little bundle of fluff into my arms. Looking into her face, twelve-week-old Gracie reminded me of our old friend Barney who had recently died. We never did get to see the kennels; it felt as if we were meant to have Gracie and that she had been waiting for us.

If none of the animals feel right, be patient and return another day or try different centres or places. In the meantime do not be surprised if a stray that remains unclaimed turns up at your door, or a desperate colleague says that his sister is going abroad suddenly leaving a homeless dog, cat, bird or rabbit.

CHOOSING THE RIGHT NAME

It is hard to choose a name in advance, because animal personalities are evident even in a kitten, foal or puppy. We know the instant we meet an animal whether we have Sabre, the tiger, or Ming, an aristocrat, even if the ball of fluff is only a few centimetres all round.

Rescue animals may have been given a name by the centre, but they are usually amenable to a change if you add your chosen name to the one that has been previously used for a week or so and then gradually drop the first name.

Anything can prompt a name, the colour of the animal – Misty or Honey – or a personality trait, such as Lightning for an animal that leaps around all day. But often you – or your partner or child – may speak an unplanned name together when you first see the animal and in that split second you will know it could not be anything else. On pages 170–80 I have listed the names of all kinds of animals and birds with brief meanings, and you may like to look through these to see which best fits your pet. Many a Bandito was so named for running off with the family dinner within five minutes of arrival.

More pendulum power

The pendulum is another good method if a name does not instantly come to mind or you like several equally. Write the names on slips of paper and place them in a circle on the floor. Slowly pass the pendulum clockwise around the circle of names and it will pull down over one of them. Although this might be the one you had not considered as a favourite, as you get to know your pet you will discover how appropriate your unconscious choice was.

In the next chapter we will look at the apparently inexplicable and yet common telepathic bond between owner and pet and discover ways of strengthening the bond.

3 | Communicating intuitively with your pet

THERE IS NO DOUBT that telepathy – unspoken communication between pets and humans – comes from the deep bond of love and loyalty between pet and owner. Some of the day-to-day incidents in the lives of animals and humans are quite remarkable and yet pass unnoticed because they are so commonplace.

Barbara, an English south-coast businesswoman, told me that when she was a child living in Liverpool her two dogs would go into the hall and wait patiently five minutes before her father walked through the front door. Barbara's father worked on the ferry crossings to Ireland and would come home at different times after irregular periods of absence. As a steward, he was able to bring home leftovers as titbits for his pets.

How could the animals have known when he would arrive? The conscious mind has strong analytical powers, but these are only the tip of the iceberg. Those powers that we often call psychic are not usually amenable to formal testing because they are spontaneous and cannot be repeated in a laboratory. What seems more certain, however, is that what we call enduring emotions, such as love and loyalty, do act as the channel for this ability.

It is not only dogs that are able to tune in to an owner's movements. Valerie who lives in Maldon in Essex described:

When I was young I used to walk three and a half miles home from school. Steve, my stallion, used to whinny when I crossed the railway line and was still about ten minutes' walk away and so, of course, he could not see me. My mother would put the kettle on when she heard the whinny, as she knew I would not be long. I used to hear Steve whinnying in my mind's ear as I crossed the railway.

Steve and I always had a psychic link. Once I was sitting indoors and I knew something was wrong with him. I went out to the paddock and saw that Steve had his tether caught around his legs.

Bev, from Home Rescue (see page 8), was so intrigued by this seemingly psychic connection that she decided to test her dog Sprout. She described: 'On three separate occasions I asked Sprout in my head if he wanted to come to the shops. I did not move a muscle and it was not the usual time to go out. Each time he pricked up his ears and went to wait at the door.'

As I mentioned in the Introduction, the Cambridge bio-chemist Dr Rupert Sheldrake has investigated this phenomena successfully. Dr Sheldrake carried out random household surveys of dog owners and discovered that 46 per cent of dog owners in England and 45 per cent in California claimed that their animal anticipates the return of a member of the household, by waiting for him or her at a door, window, driveway or a bus stop. In both surveys, most of the dogs that anticipated the return of a family member did so less than five minutes before the person arrived home. However, 16 per cent of the dog owners interviewed in England and 19 per cent in California said that their dogs reacted more than ten minutes before the human arrived.

Explanations that the animal picks up cues from others in the home or that it learns the routine do not apply in cases where the owner does not have a set routine and where members of the family are unaware of the precise time of the return home. Rationalisation remains elusive.

WHAT IS THE POINT OF THESE LINKS?

Telepathic powers in humans have been widely observed between mothers and children of all ages and often described as maternal intuition. For animals, at a practical level, the two-way connection means that we can learn to send messages to our pets to reassure them if we are late or unexpectedly away from home.

REASSURING OUR PETS WHEN WE ARE NOT WITH THEM

Though these links are by their nature spontaneous, you can use telepathy or directed thoughts to reassure a pet if you are unexpectedly late, if you are ill and cannot visit your horse at the stable or if you have to be away from home and will leave the animal with a sitter or at kennels. I have also found this helpful if an animal has to stay overnight at the vet and you cannot be with him or her. The method is simple:

1 When you need to contact the animal, try to find a few moments alone in a quiet place wherever you may be.

2 You can focus on your pet by establishing a physical connection that you always carry with you; for example, you might like to keep a tiny locket with some hair from the animal or a small photograph that you can hold when you need to contact the animal. As you become more experienced at routine telepathic communication with your pet you will not need the physical connection.

3 Sit down and imagine yourself and the animal in a familiar setting with the animal just in front of you.

4 Begin by picturing a section of the animal's fur or feathers and gradually allow the image to expand in your mind so that you build up the entire animal, ending with the head and the ears.

5 Look into the eyes of the invisible animal and smile. You may *see* in your mind the animal's eyes light up with pleasure.

6 Now imagine in your ear the sound your pet makes when he or she is contented, purring, whinnying or snuffling. Gradually turn up the volume in your head so it excludes all other sounds.

7 Softly call the animal's name and any endearments you frequently use. If you are in company, do this in your mind. Repeat this over and over so it becomes a mantra, and then pass on your message; for example, 'Home soon' or 'You are safe'.

8 Finally, extend your fingers and imagine the fur or feathers as you run your hands through it, and the soft place behind the ears. If you are alone, stroke the imaginary fur, speaking words of reassurance and telling the animal you will soon be together.

If you want to test this power, ask someone to be with the animal while you are away and take a note of the time you make your psychic contact. Ask the person who is with the animal if it reacted unusually at that time.

BECOMING AWARE OF DANGER TELEPATHICALLY

As you develop the link, you will find you can easily access the spontaneous innate power of knowing instinctively when any creature with whom you have a deep bond of affection is in danger, hurt or distressed, even if you are not with him or her. This link can even be a lifesaver. Let me give you an example. Annie, who lives in the countryside outside Adelaide in Australia, told me that she woke one night and heard the distressed meowing of her Persian cat, Mel, whom she had owned since childhood:

My parents were away. The sound was in my ear, right next to me on the bed. But when I awoke I realised Mel was not on the bed. When I searched, Mel was not even in the house, though I could still hear her calling as though in distress. I realised eventually that the sound was coming from the garden and, grabbing a torch, I followed her distressed yowls, calling to her that I was on my way. I followed the sound through the gate into bush land and trees for about half a mile.

At last I found her trapped in some barbed wire that was caught round her mouth. Some stupid kids had obviously tried to make an animal snare. I managed to free her and carried her to the house where I called the vet. Mel made a full recovery. But afterwards I realised there was no way she could have called me with that wire round her jaw and anyway it was too far from the house for the sound to have carried. Dad said I must have been dreaming and was just lucky to find Mel. Mum believed me, but said not to tell other people as they would think I was crazy.

Like Valerie with her horse, Annie heard the sound intuitively. During my research into this phenomenon I have discovered similar stories and have found that most people do not talk about them except to other pet lovers who have had similar experiences themselves. I have found in industrial societies particularly that if an occurrence like Annie's can't be explained logically then it tends to be considered as impossible or untrue.

THE TWO-WAY BOND

This telepathic link works in two ways so that an animal can save the life of an owner by picking up silent cries for help that the owner cannot make out loud. Even more surprising is that an animal can show amazing initiative. Some of these instances, described officially as examples of animal instinct, can make front-page news.

Of course, animals do have highly developed physical senses, but the following story is hard to explain in terms of normal instinctive responses. The incident happened on

27 December 1997 when 12-year-old Misty became separated from her family on a walk through the forest close to the canyon of the Buffalo River in a wild area of Arkansas. Although a police helicopter and 100 trackers with trained bloodhounds were desperately combing the area, it was Scotty, the family's mongrel, who discovered Misty and remained with her as she wandered deeper into the forest, cold and unable to find her bearings. Misty was not found until the morning and would almost certainly have died in the sub-zero temperatures had Scotty not kept her warm with his body and awake by continuously barking.

Scotty found her when even trained bloodhounds and trackers could not. The difference, I would suggest, is that the link of love enables animals to find or save us using senses beyond even their normally acute physiological ones. On occasions the animals appear to display almost human reasoning powers in response to an owner's danger.

Take the case of Margaret, who on 23 August 2001 became very ill in the middle of the night at her residential home in Fife in Scotland. Her condition meant she was unable to call for help. However, her cat, Gandalf, continued to tug at the emergency cord until help came. Gandalf's actions are inexplicable in terms of mere physiological or personal survival responses. But there may be much more to animal personalities than is conventionally understood.

A similarly amazing story comes from Kansas City in America. In February 1998, Mike was alone except for Brandi, his spaniel, replacing the wheel on the family car. Suddenly the car fell on top of Mike, trapping him beneath it. Brandi instinctively understood the danger and ran into the house unprompted, fetched the phone in his mouth and pushed it into the hand of his owner who was able to dial 911 for help.

ARE PETS TUNED IN TO OUR WAVELENGTH?

I would suggest that one explanation for this behaviour also relates to mothers and children. The automatic radar I spoke of that attracts us to a particular animal is like sensitive antennae emanating from a person who cares for another person. As the attachment grows, so the antennae between two or more people, for example a pet and his owner, become tuned in to the needs of the other on a deeply unconscious level. So if your own protective mechanism is off duty, for example if you are asleep or feeling very ill, your pet's protective mechanism will still be alert and watching out for you. So, by perhaps using the same channels it is somehow able to respond with what appear to be human reasoning powers (for example, I need to fetch the phone). This theory might explain the telepathic attachment between the assistance dog, Endal, and his owner Alan, and Endal's ability to anticipate Alan's needs (see page xv). This ultimately may lead to the question of whether animals are evolved spiritual creatures, and I talk of this more on page 118.

Psychic games

If your animal seems slow to respond to your unspoken thoughts, psychic games can fine-tune the connection. Dogs tend to be most responsive to psychic games, although cats also respond well, especially if they have been in the household from the time they were kittens and are the only pet. Horses, rabbits (especially house ones), guinea pigs that are handled frequently and birds, such as parrots or budgerigars, can also be amenable, and you can adapt the suggestions for dogs below quite easily. Begin with a really simple psychic game.

Let's go for a walk/feed you

1 Work at a time when you would not normally exercise or feed your dog.

2 Sit facing away from the dog and keep your hands in your lap, so that you do not accidentally look towards

the door or make a slight movement as if you were rising from your seat.

3 Make sure there are no other people or distractions, such as loud noise.

4 Relax and clear your mind.

5 In your mind, picture yourself going to the door and getting the lead and then the two of you romping off for a walk, or yourself filling the food bowl with favourite treats. Visualising the scene works because animals respond better to pictures than words.

6 Keep visualising the sequence, and before long the dog should go to the door or to the food bowl, or it may start looking round for you and greeting you.

7 Reward the dog with a treat even if he or she does not make the connection.

8 Persevere at regular intervals and in time you may just need to begin imagining the actions and will not need to finish the sequence to make the dog respond.

Come to me

This time you are going to practise calling the dog to you without speaking any words.

1 Wait until the dog is settled in another part of the house.

2 Sit quietly for a few minutes so the dog does not pick up movement with its acute senses, and then call his or her name two or three times in your mind as though you were speaking out loud.

3 Pause for a minute and then repeat the call.

4 Continue until the dog comes, and reward him or her.

This also works well with birds or horses: they may call out, rattle the cage door or come to the stable door. You can stand hidden from view with these creatures while you play the game.

Which bowl?

This involves two identical bowls of food at feeding time. The results could be achieved by chance but not if you consistently guide the dog to the chosen bowl with your thoughts.

1 Fill both bowls while the dog cannot see you and then decide which one you are going to direct the dog to.

2 Sit still and face slightly away from the bowls so that your eyes or hands do not give off unconscious signals. Call or fetch the dog and then visualise it going to the chosen bowl. Even if it heads for the other one initially you may be able to visualise it changing course.

3 Over a period of a month, keep a note of the number of times you are correct, and you will be surprised how rapidly the scores improve if you carry out the test regularly.

Phone home

You can try this with any creature that shares your home, though dogs and cats tend to be the most responsive.

1 Choose the family member to whom the dog is closest.

2 Ask the person to phone twice during the day at unspecified times so that you will not react in an unusual way.

3 Ask that he or she talks about the dog during the conversation, but be sure only to reply 'yes' and 'no' and do not refer to the dog or caller by name.

4 See if the dog goes towards the phone or becomes excited during the call when that person rings. The dog may react even before the receiver is picked up.

I'm coming home

Again, this is best with house creatures. It is useful for an animal to be able to anticipate your return so that he or she will not fret if you are delayed, and this is a good way to build up a connection with them. The game will open the floodgates to trust and affection.

1 You will need someone who can observe the dog. You will also need two watches or clocks – one for each of you. Ask the observer to note down the time the dog appears to anticipate your arrival, such as by waiting at the door or gate.

2 Do not tell the observer the precise time you intend to be home. Ten minutes before you are due to arrive, call the dog in your mind, mentally pat it and tell it you will be home very soon.

3 Note the time. Call the dog again in your mind five minutes before you reach home.

4 When you arrive home note if the dog is waiting in the hall or by the gate and you can ask the observer what time the dog took up that position.

5 Vary the time on different days and try the experiment once or twice a week for about three months and see if a pattern emerges.

Find the ball

This is quite a complicated game and will only work with a dog (or occasionally a very intelligent cat) that you have owned for some time and with which you have built up strong telepathic communication. Treat the game as fun. If it does not work, it merely means that the animal does not enjoy the game and it is not a reflection of the depth of your relationship.

1 Work either in the garden or a fenced-off area, or in an area of the home that is relatively uncluttered.

2 Use three or four hiding places to hide the ball; for example, under a rug or inside a cardboard box. Clear all other obstacles or possible hiding places.

3 Have a few daily trial runs to familiarise the dog with the technique; for example, hiding the ball under a rug and saying to the dog, 'Find the ball', then lifting an object where it is not and saying, 'No' and then going to the rug and saying, 'Here'.

4 Then practise the full test (below), but go with the dog and help it to find the ball.

5 The full test: show the dog the ball, ask a friend or family member to shield the dog's eyes and hide the ball and say, 'Ball gone'.

6 Now say, 'Find the ball', and picture where the ball is in your mind (images are easier than words for dogs).

7 Concentrate really strongly on the hidden object. At first the dog may just choose at random. Praise him anyway.

8 If the dog is wrong, show the correct hiding place and say, 'Here's the ball'.

9 Over time the dog should tune in to your unspoken instructions to find the hiding place more rapidly.

IF YOU HATE TESTS

You should not feel you have to test yourself or the animal unless you want to. Some people find that intuitive links work best in real situations where there is an actual need, whether demonstrating the psychic link between humans or between humans and animals.

TELEPATHIC BONDS THAT CAN CALL YOUR PET HOME

Wild creatures have an amazing homing instinct; for example, we know that salmon find their way hundreds or even thousands of miles to their original spawning place, and there are countless tales of wartime carrier pigeons taking messages back to the base through enemy fire even when injured. One explanation is that the creature's instinctive radar is tuned not to a person in these instances, but a place.

With a pet, however, the telepathic bond is tuned in to its owner, and it operates even over great distances regardless of whether the pet has ever been to the place where the owner is. This is one plausible explanation for the remarkable journey of Deni, the dog, that had been left behind when his owner, Goran Radanovic, escaped from Petrinja, 30 miles south-east of Zagreb during the Yugoslav conflict. Four and a half months later, in January 1995, Deni arrived at the refugee camp in Ruma, 50 miles north of Belgrade, where his owner was staying. Deni had walked more than 300 miles across unknown territory through the bitterly cold Balkan winter.

So why do pet animals and birds get lost if we have this telepathic link to guide them? Some pets can have their instincts blunted if they get too comfortable and rely on the owner to keep them safe. Working with the intuitive bond can help to awaken a pet that is less than tuned in, and I have made suggestions throughout the book of ways you can do this. Alternatively, even a tuned-in pet may panic if it accidentally strays, or if the pet has been stolen and abandoned miles away or ill-treated by abductors or strangers while it is wandering.

Of course, sometimes an animal may choose to go missing if it objects to a new human or animal family member. This is especially the case with cats, who may also dislike a house move or simply have wanderlust that overrides domesticity. In such cases, attempts to find the creature fail and we sometimes have to let go emotionally, though with regret.

Some people believe that we can kick-start a creature's homing instinct if it is not fully functioning by calling to them telepathically. This will draw the pet back to us. So even if a search fails, a creature may turn up the next day, having responded to our psychic call.

HOW TO FIND A LOST ANIMAL OR BIRD

Use the ever-valuable pendulum as your psychic antennae to tune in to the animal or bird wherever it might be. Whereas emotion increases the psychic link, panic can sometimes make it hard to listen to your inner radar; the pendulum movement will stop you second-guessing or trying to imagine the likely location of the pet. Those of you who own pets will know they will be in the least likely place.

1 Hold the pendulum chain between your thumb and first finger so that the pendulum can swing freely but does not veer wildly with the slightest movement.

2 Before you begin searching, establish the vital positive/negative response, i.e. which way the pendulum swings for 'yes' and 'no' when you ask the question, 'Is this the right way?' You can do this by thinking of a happy situation, in which case the pendulum will generally swing in a clockwise circle or ellipse to show you the positive/right-way response.

3 To establish the negative/wrong-way pendulum response, think of something sad and the pendulum will generally make an anticlockwise circle or ellipse.

4 You can initially hold the pendulum over a very detailed map of your area until it circles clockwise or even pulls down over one section. This reduces walking time, as it will indicate the locality of the missing creature. (Expert dowsers have found oil and wells by using a map in this way.)

5 Before you begin walking, visualise your pet coming towards you and softly call his or her name. Then let your mind go blank except for the question, 'Is this the right way?'

6 Start walking, and stop when the pendulum begins to circle anticlockwise. This shows you are going off-track. Retrace your steps until it begins to circle clockwise again.

7 The circling will become faster as you approach the spot where the animal is hiding or has become trapped, and it may begin to spin round and round very fast, first in one direction and then the other, outside a shed or outbuilding or near some bushes.

8 Call the animal's name out loud. He or she may be asleep, exhausted, or so frightened that there may be no immediate response, so persevere.

9 If you still hear nothing but the pendulum is still spinning, knock on doors and ask politely if you might search any outbuildings for your animal.

10 If you begin to doubt your judgement, take a rest and return to where you lost the trail.

If the pendulum does not respond at all, it may be that the pet has died or left the area. Or, indeed, does not wish to be found. Continue to use conventional means to try to find the animal, but also listen to your heart: it will tell you when a pet is not going to return. However, you might have created a psychic link by focusing on the animal or bird and it may return spontaneously shortly afterwards.

In the next chapter we will examine the strange but quite common phenomena of animals and birds that are somehow able to go beyond the linear time barrier and see into the future.

4 | Can animals see into the future?

ANIMALS SOMETIMES SEEM AWARE of events before they happen. This may be because, unlike humans, their minds are not limited to strictly linear time or it may be because they are so sensitive that they are able to pick up early warning signals of danger on their automatic radar before human radar can tune in.

Physiological explanations, even accounting for the acute senses of animals, are certainly not the whole story. An animal's sight, sense and hearing are certainly more acute than a human's, but this does not fully explain how a pet can anticipate danger to the owner sometimes hours or even days before it occurs. Take the example of Donna, a retriever, owned by Sture who lives in Halland, a village in Sweden. Donna always slept in the stable to guard the horse from intruders. However, on the night of 9 January 1998, she ran into the house and refused to sleep or settle. That same night the house caught fire while Sture was asleep on the sofa. Donna barked continuously and tugged at Sture's ear until he awoke. He managed to break a window and escape minutes before the house was completely engulfed in flames. The stable was undamaged.

Coincidence? Like humans who have premonitions that often involve a close relation or friend, the dog changed an established behaviour pattern for no apparent reason and saved her owner's life as a result. As with the telepathic bond it may well be that links of deep affection and loyalty form channels through which these forewarnings operate.

An equally amazing story comes from Cathedral City in California. In 1998, a normally obedient Welsh corgi, called Duke, dragged his 85-year-old owner, Jack, away from the kerb, barking, pulling at his leash and stopping Jack from crossing the road. Seconds later a truck came hurtling round on the wrong side of the road and missed Jack by inches. It was a noisy area with roadworks so even a dog's acute hearing and vision would not have been fully operational. And how could the animal have known that the truck was coming on the wrong side of the road?

Because incidents such as these are one-offs in dramatic circumstances they are even less amenable to testing than telepathic incidents. However, in greater and lesser degrees humans ignore their pets' warnings at their peril. Of course animals' and birds' warnings tend to come in the form of persistent howling, yowling or screeching without apparent reason and so are not always easy to interpret. But with patience and time the cause may become clear.

LISTENING TO YOUR ANIMALS

The unprompted howling of dogs without reason is almost worldwide, and has been considered a warning to humans throughout the ages. Lesley, who lives on the Isle of Wight in the UK, believes that if she had listened to her dogs' warning when they howled inconsolably before she left home one morning she could have averted a potential disaster. She told me:

> Ten years ago I was living in Donegal in Ireland and had two young sister dogs. They were cross-Labradors. I also had an older cat, Flicka, that my husband and I had brought from England and which was very special to me.

Each morning my husband drove me in the car three miles to the nearest town where I caught the bus to Derry across the border where I worked.

I was sitting in the car at about nine o'clock one morning waiting for my husband to get in the car. As usual he was fussing around indoors. Suddenly the dogs started howling. They had never done that before. They were used to being left and had each other for company. I felt very uneasy about going to work. I could still hear them howling as we drove down the road.

At 4.30 p.m. I arrived in the town and rang my husband to tell him to pick me up. When he met me he said: 'I have some bad news for you. The cat has been run over in the road.' It was a very quiet area with few cars and she was a very intelligent cat. I'm sure the dogs knew that something bad was going to happen that day. I have always felt that if I had listened to them and not gone to work I might have been able to save her.

EVERYDAY WARNINGS FROM PETS

Most warnings from animals and birds are not of the life-and-death kind but they can alert us to hazards we would sooner avoid, nevertheless. Here are a few to watch out for:

- If you are buying a new house or apartment and there are no birds flying around outside, you know that there is something not quite right about the place. Proceed cautiously.

- If possible, introduce an animal briefly to a new home before signing the final deeds. If the animal refuses to enter the house or to go into certain rooms, find out a little more before going ahead. The house may have negative earth energies, an unfriendly ghost or just be so full of unhappy memories you would never settle.

- If a normally friendly pet takes an instant dislike to a stranger or acquaintance, be wary and do not leave the stranger alone in rooms in your home or agree to meet in a quiet place. A parrot that squawks incessantly when a particular person comes to the house, or that acts aggressively may be picking up hidden signals that all is not well.

ANIMALS' PREDICTIVE POWERS AND HEALTH

I have already mentioned how the protective feelings animals have for owners seem to enable them to predict impending danger to their owner. Animals can also alert owners with chronic health problems to the onset of an attack. Although much of the evidence is anecdotal it has been increasingly accepted by health professionals. Joan, who lives in Brighton in East Sussex, has bad asthma. Her husband regularly has to be away from home at night leaving her alone with her dog. Heidi, a dog adopted as a puppy by Joan from a rescue centre, stays at Joan's side while she is asleep and if she detects a change in Joan's breathing pattern, she nudges Joan awake. This enables Joan to use her inhaler, thus preventing a more serious attack.

On both sides of the Atlantic, it has been discovered that dogs can anticipate epileptic seizures in their owners up to 30 minutes before a seizure occurs, and so act as an advance warning system. Jacki, who lives in Lancashire in the UK and who has a son suffering from epilepsy, discovered this power in her own dog quite by chance. When she was woken by her Labrador, Lugo, barking in the early hours of the morning, Jacki at first thought there was a burglar in the house. She and her husband John investigated, but found nothing. Eventually, the dog seized Jacki's dressing gown and dragged her upstairs to her son Brian's bedroom. Here she discovered Brian, who suffers from epilepsy, in the middle of a major seizure.

After this incident, Jacki realised that Brian needed his own dog to be his personal watch-pet, so Jacki bought a puppy trained by Support Dogs in Sheffield. Brian now has far more freedom to play with his friends without constant supervision, as his dog can give between 15 and 20 minutes' warning before he is affected. This gives Brian time to come home and sit down and for his mother to get his medication ready and make sure he is in a safe place. If Brian does not heed his pet's warning in time, his pet will sit on his feet and stop him from walking until he listens to her.

In practice, however, only a proportion of trained dogs give warnings of epileptic seizures. In 1998 Roger Reep, a neuroscientist at the College of Veterinarian Medicine at the University of Florida, and a colleague, Deb Dalziel, interviewed about 70 subjects suffering from epilepsy. They discovered that 5 per cent of the sample who owned dogs confirmed that the dogs alerted them before the onset of a seizure. According to Dr Mike Sapp, of Paws With a Cause in Michigan, who also studied the phenomenon, a close bond with the owner as well as the sensitivity of the individual dog are major factors.

Michael Goehring, executive programme director of the Great Plains Assistance Dogs Foundation in Jud, North Dakota, believes that all dogs may have this ability, but only a small number have the appropriate personality to use it. The trigger for the ability is not fully understood, although some experts believe that dogs may be able to sense subtle physiological changes – perhaps through their acute sense of smell – in the patient prior to an epileptic fit which the patient or other humans present are unable to detect.

PETS AS NIGHT NURSES

Even in less dramatic events, pets frequently seem to be aware of times when a family member is ill, and they may try to alert us. If a pet wakes you unusually in the night and seems to be taking you towards a family member's bedroom, look in on all small children or very elderly or chronically sick relatives. There have been a number of recorded cases of animals alerting owners to a sick child or even to a baby who has kicked off the blankets; animals are surprisingly sensitive to even minor health changes.

ANIMALS THAT SAVE OTHER ANIMALS

Animals also show strong predictive powers towards the danger of other creatures, especially their offspring. Perhaps this should not be surprising, as such protectiveness may come from the physical connection that the mother has through carrying her young in her body during pregnancy. This closeness lingers after the birth, especially while she is feeding her young. So when a sense of danger builds up, the mother, whether human or animal, is momentarily able to step outside the normal constraints of what is possible.

For almost 15 years, I have been studying maternal intuition and how its power seems to transcend time barriers when a child is in danger. You might be interested to read some of my findings in *The Mother Link* (Ulysses Press, Berkeley, California, 1999). I have also found that animals seem to have especially pronounced predictive instincts in connection with their young. A verified experience was reported during the Second World War in London concerning Faith, a tabby and white stray cat that was adopted as a stray kitten by the rector of St Augustine's Church, in Watling Street. She lived in the rectory that was next to the church.

In early September 1940, Faith gave birth to Panda, a black and white kitten, and was caring for it in a room at the top of the four-storey house. Towards the end of the month Faith became agitated and, having searched the house, carried the kitten to a ground floor room on the other side. The rector, thinking the animals were safer upstairs, took the kitten back to the original room, but Faith immediately carried the kitten downstairs again. After four or five fruitless attempts the rector admitted defeat.

Three nights afterwards a bomb hit the roof of the rectory and destroyed the whole building. The rector searched for the cat and found her shielding her kitten among the rubble. In spite of heavy bombing the church was not damaged so the rector took Faith and her kitten to the church vestry where Faith settled in spite of the noise and flames outside. Had the animals been on the upper floor they would not have survived. The cat changed her behaviour seemingly without reason. She had experienced bombing in the area before and not panicked previously, and she had happily kept the kitten upstairs until just prior to the direct hit.

In his research into psychic animals, Dr Rupert Sheldrake discovered a number of accounts of wartime animals that acted strangely before a bomb landed, long before they would have detected any physical vibrations.

ANIMALS THAT PREDICT EARTHQUAKES

Vibrations may also partially explain another common example of predictive powers in the animal kingdom; animals and birds can give warning of earthquakes before humans or even complex instruments have any indication of impending disaster. This may partly be a physical reaction to electrical or magnetic changes, especially if the creatures are close to the epicentre of the impending earthquakes.

Again there is a historical precedent: the most common warning of an impending earthquake reported since the time of the ancient Greeks is that bees swarm from their hives. Derek Acorah, the medium and psychic researcher who has studied the phenomenon in modern times, commented:

> Before the earthquake in Morocco in 1960, stray animals, including dogs, were seen streaming from the port before the shock that killed 15,000 people. A similar phenomenon was observed three years later before an earthquake reduced the city of Skopje, Yugoslavia, to rubble. Most animals seemed to have left before the quake. The Russians observed too that animals began to abandon Tashkent before the 1966 earthquake.

From my own research I have discovered that in both China and Japan this early warning system is taken very seriously, and on 4 February 1975 the Chinese cleared the city of Haicheng because of signs of unusually disturbed animal behaviour. A few hours later an earthquake measuring 7.3 on the Richter scale hit the area. Although there was extensive damage to buildings, it is estimated that 90,000 lives were saved because the animals' early warning system was recognised.

Even deep-sea fish are affected by pre-earthquake panic, and shoals of fish, especially catfish, have been observed leaping out of the water prior to a quake.

These animal warnings can occur anything up to a week or more before an earthquake, though they are most dramatic during the 24 hours before the quake strikes. Perhaps we should not be surprised, for animals and birds are so in tune with the earth that, if we allow them to, they can alert us to all kinds of changes, from adverse weather conditions to volcanic eruptions and tidal waves.

TRUSTING ANIMAL INSTINCTS

Though few animals may be regularly as psychically sensitive as the ones I have described in this chapter, almost every animal displays some predictive powers that can alert you to a less than friendly atmosphere or even potential danger. There are practical ways we can use our pet's extrasensory perception. Watch for sudden disturbances in an animal's behaviour that are different from normal crankiness or attention-seeking behaviour. The key is if the behaviour is unusual for the animal or bird; for example, if a dog scratches on the door to go out in the night, that may be nothing unusual. However, if an animal wakes you and is obviously agitated or keeps pawing at you, then that indicates your creature wishes to tell you something. First of all follow where the animal leads you. If there is nothing obvious, check for disturbances outside or fire hazards. Lock any unbolted doors and take out electric plugs – just in case.

If you are at the beach with a normally beach-loving dog or horse that suddenly attempts to leave, it may be detecting some earth energy, such as unusually high waves moving inshore or an impending windstorm, so trust your weather wizard. Horses are especially sensitive to detecting future danger, so if you are out riding and a horse that is normally amenable refuses to go ahead or wants to go back to the stables, go with the animal's instincts. You may never know if the animal was right, but at least you may have avoided a potential hazard.

Of course none of this is new and for thousands of years people have been listening to animals and birds for warnings or advice. Let's look at a historical precedent.

PROPHETIC CREATURES FROM THE PAST

Historically, the predictive abilities of animals and birds have been acknowledged and even used in divination systems to predict future events. The Roman historian Livy tells how during the fourth century BCE, geese cackled in the courtyard of a temple when the Gauls sent scouts to the city under cover of darkness to climb Capitol Hill; thanks to the geese the city was saved. They responded when human guards did not. Since there would have been movement in the city even at night, what could it have been that alerted the geese to the presence of those few invaders?

So seriously did the Romans take the predictive powers of animals, and especially birds, that they used cockerels and hens to provide answers to questions posed to them by senators and generals as well as ordinary people. A circle would be drawn on the ground and divided into sections, which would then be labelled with letters or special signs indicating a particular decision. Corn was then added to each section. The birds first appeared to peck the corn at random, but in fact the sections from which they pecked corn spelled out a significant name or message that answered the question posed. Roman legionnaires would carry these divinatory fowl with them in cages on their travels.

The ancient Egyptians believed Apis, the sacred bull of Memphis, near Cairo, to be an earthly manifestation of the creator god Ptah. They would ask him questions and would make decisions about which battle action to take according to whether he accepted or rejected food or which pen he chose to enter. The ancient Egyptians and Romans were highly evolved civilisations and presumably these methods must have been sufficiently accurate for them to survive among battle-weary generals. Written evidence from Egyptian papyri and accounts of Roman conquests by such distinguished authors as the Emperor Caesar witness that animal and bird oracles were used during the last millennia BCE in Egypt and throughout the time of the Roman Empire. Even today, street vendors in India still follow the ancient practice of using a bird as a prophetic creature. They use a parrot or other exotic bird to select letters or a yes/no response to indicate the name of a lover.

If you have relatively tame ducks or hens you can follow the Roman method exactly, but other creatures may be more accessible and just as effective as seers.

You do not need to ask a question concerning your animal; you can request help on any decision you need to make about the future, however trivial. You can also use this method so that an animal or bird might choose its name from a selection of names you like (see pages 170–180). Children love to watch this.

The response from dogs is the best, as cats tend to be too independent and rabbits lack concentration. Horses are good subjects, as are birds, such as parrots, budgerigars, canaries and cockatiels, if they are handled regularly and fly freely.

DECISION-MAKING USING A PET

On an everyday level too, you can use your pet to help you to make decisions including, for example, a possible holiday location by using pictures of hotels or resorts cut from a brochure. You can also write words or symbols on pieces of paper to indicate options; for example, 'speak out', 'seek advice', 'remain silent' or 'take action'. Below I have suggested how I think this oracle method works. Although you are unlikely to make a major life change on the strength of an apparently random choice by your pet, your mind can use a decision suggested by the animal to bring up all kinds of thoughts and alternatives that you can then use in your final decision.

1 This experiment is best tried after your pet has had a light meal. Write a number of options, names or pictures representing the choices on separate slips of paper, and place them in a circle several centimetres (inches) apart.

2 Set the same kind of small treat, biscuit or chew on each option.

3 Have one person distract the animal or bird while you are setting up the circle and then place it in the centre of the circle, turning it gently two or three times so it does not go to the first option it sees on entering. If you are using a horse, make a larger circle of treats and lead him or her around it. A bird can peck seed from tiny dishes under which the paper slips are placed.

4 Usually, even a greedy animal will not wolf down all the treats, but will sniff a number of them before choosing one.

5 After the choice is made, allow the animal to eat the other treats if he or she wishes.

6 If the animal rejects them all, collect the papers and treats, putting just one treat on the food bowl as a reward for co-operating.

7 Try the next day with different names or options.

ANIMAL AND BIRD ORACLES

In ancient Greek and Roman augury the study of the movements of wild birds was also taken very seriously as a method of predicting future events and the best courses of action. Indeed crow divination is still practised in parts of India. We also can use this knowledge, but how can the movements of birds or animals relate to our personal lives, and more importantly how can they alert us to matters not accessible to our conscious mind or predictable using the evidence currently available? One way is to interpret the significance of different movements made by certain creatures at a particular time, using the set meanings that have been given to the movements and proved reliable over the centuries. These meanings will act as a basic template or framework which will indicate particular areas of our life that need attention or about which we have doubts or unanswered questions.

Our unconscious minds can then flesh out and adapt this template with knowledge that is not accessible to the conscious mind using symbols that are triggered within us by the divinatory process we are undertaking. This will then become a valuable psychological device for prompting our highly knowledgeable but relatively inaccessible stores of knowledge to work.

This is based on the premise, as expressed by the psychotherapist Jung, that no action is accidental or random. Therefore, by using psychokinesis or mind power (see Bird augury on pages 44–50) we can somehow influence where the birds we are focusing on will fly or land simply by concentrating on them. This basic information can give us clues about the best possible path to follow or decision to be made.

Even if you do not believe such psychic influence is possible over a particular aspect of nature, you can still use bird divination as a way of focusing your thoughts and accessing the hidden wisdom that we all possess to find the correct course. Put another way, the questioner's unconscious wisdom already knows the correct course but is unable to convey this to the conscious mind except through an outward sign (such as when we used the pendulum to help us).

Observing bird flight is only the first part of the process, and the experience opens a doorway to the seeker's deeper wisdom that has been awakened by focusing on the experience and suspending logic for just a few moments. It is like switching from the left, logical side of the brain to the more intuitive area on the right. Either during or after the event, images or words may appear in your mind, perhaps while you are walking home or during a dream at night. So what appears to be a basic fortune-telling message is expanded in the seeker's mind or explained in the dream or on the daydreaming plane.

You may like to try the methods below. At the worst they will give you an hour's entertainment – and as a bonus set off those elusive hidden thought processes.

Bird augury

The more you learn about birds and the way they behave, the more easily you can combine natural observation with prophetic (or intuitive) powers. In this way, if a bird or flock of birds act strangely then you may be able to deduce that they know something you do not about changes in the weather or an impending natural event; farmers and those who work on the land are often gifted in *reading* animal patterns and many are expert meteorologists.

Bird augury works on the principle that birds are closer to nature than humans and therefore more sensitive to invisible energies. Therefore, their physical actions express approaching prevailing energy – such as earthquakes – before even the most psychic human is aware of it. Variables include the kinds of birds – assuming there is normally a variety in your garden or wherever you are working (see page 46, Bird divination in practice, for different bird strengths) – their call or song, the size of the group, how and where they fly and land at the moment you ask your question and whether this differs from the way they would normally act (see below).

Moving beyond fortune-telling

As I said earlier, the whole process is far subtler than it seems if you take those principles literally (I have listed the traditional meanings below). As in all forms of divination, it is the feeling you experience deep inside in response to an external omen that is the key to gaining knowledge.

Spontaneous bird appearances can also have meaning. In all the official and generalised interpretations of bird augury through the ages, an owl tapping on the window is interpreted as foretelling the death of an emperor or at least a difficult period for the residents of the house. But dig deeper; this unusual phenomenon (tapping on your window) may be pointing out to you that the answer to your problem is very close if you just open your eyes: an owl tapping suggests you should ask someone wise – and close to you – for help.

Beginning bird divination

You can practise bird divination with absolutely any birds you see anywhere. But like any good augur of old, you will want your personal flock, so from the beginning, it is quite important to build up your connection with the birds with which you will be working most often. These could be pigeons and starlings in a town square, sparrows in the garden, seabirds on the shore or on urban playing fields and near reservoirs on land, the geese in a local wildlife sanctuary or birds in a park in a place where they are frequently fed.

If possible set up a bird table or two in your garden or position a feeder to one side of a balcony to encourage birds to visit. Feed the birds regularly in your chosen place. Sit and observe them in the early morning, in the midday sunshine and in the evening. That way you will know if their behaviour is unusual. Flocks of pigeons are especially effective for divination, as they are often composed of birds of many different shades and they are constantly landing and fluttering off. This will give you a readily available, large selection of birds on which you can base your predictions. I have a number of distinctive thrushes and blackbirds that will come and sit on my steps every morning until I feed them. If they are absent or will not come down to be fed, the day definitely needs to be lived with caution.

Close your eyes and translate the birdcalls. An afternoon in a bird park, listening to every species, from parrots to ducks, will give you a crash course in bird speak.

Spend times also watching birds in flight through half-closed eyes, focusing on the patterns of silver and blue made by their collective energy fields or auras (see Chapter 5). In this way, you can learn to merge with the essence of the birds and so be able to obtain psychic as well as physical impressions more easily. A pair of good binoculars is essential equipment so that you can continue to monitor the birds in the sky after they have flown away.

Bird divination in practice

I have collected several rules from classical sources over the years and these will help you to interpret the birds' movements. Ask your question and then watch the birds. Using the following rules, allow images to form spontaneously in your mind as you watch the birds on the ground or in flight:

Dark and light: where there are more than one species of bird present, or differently coloured birds within the species (males and females often differ dramatically), a predominance of lighter birds landing and remaining on the ground indicates that it would be beneficial to take immediate action. Darker ones, however, suggest delay.

If you have to make a decision, the arrival or movement of a light-coloured bird would tell you to act; a darker one would tell you to wait.

Direction: birds flying in the right-hand area of the sky as you are standing or sitting indicate a smooth passage in any venture and that confident action should be taken. Birds flying on the left indicate delays, and perhaps counsel waiting or remaining silent for a while.

Birds flying straight towards the questioner indicate that happier times are coming. Those flying directly away, especially if there is no apparent reason for them suddenly taking flight, suggest that the next few days are a time for tact and caution, and for making plans rather than embarking on new ventures.

Height: the higher the flight, the more favourable will be the omen. If a bird flies directly upwards, then the venture should achieve swift success with little effort required.

If the flight is horizontal or veers up and down with the bird landing and flying off, then landing again, you may need to persevere and not be deterred by initial obstacles.

Changing course: if a bird suddenly changes direction, there may be sudden changes of heart or inconstancy from those close to you or sudden doubts of your own that you need to examine.

Hovering: if a bird hovers directly overhead – unless it is a hawk and you are standing in long grass where there may be prey – beware of hidden criticism or new friends who may be less than direct.

Birdsong: if a songbird sings or utters a cry as it takes flight, it is a good sign to go ahead at once with any matter you are considering. A bird that calls as it lands may indicate caution is needed. If a dark bird or a bird of prey screams as it circles, unless it is near to its nest there may be unexpected opposition to overcome.

Interpreting song

Dawn is a good time for listening to birdsong. Go where there are a number of birds, such as doves, blackbirds, pigeons, parrots or even crows, or best of all work with the dawn chorus in woodland or near any trees. Sunset is another time when birds are especially vocal. Ask a question and close your eyes. Let the chorus form pictures and words in your mind. Your answer will come with the flow of the song.

Agitation or serenity

Rooks skirling on their last flight of the night are a prophetic source that can be monitored over a number of nights. You can also use other flocks. Allow their calls to form words in your mind. If the birds seem agitated then change is in the air and it is a good moment to take decisive actions rather than allowing life to dictate to you. You should also avoid giving ultimatums to others. If the birds are active but serene then it indicates the overall atmosphere is one of calm. If they are sluggish, this may indicate a period of stagnation ahead or obstacles to your plans. Serene birds landing and flying off in a calm manner are a good sign of smooth times ahead. Birds that become agitated for no apparent reason may suggest sudden change or a minor panic over future plans. You may have noticed that people sometimes complain of periods when everyone seems edgy, when plans seem to go wrong for no good reason or there are a lot of accidents. This would suggest that some underlying energies are affecting almost everyone psychologically and, perhaps, physically. Birds are good at identifying these periods just in advance of them occurring.

Interpreting bird numbers

You can use numerology to interpret the meanings associated with bird numbers. Find an area where birds congregate and then follow the steps below. You can then interpret their meaning by using my list of qualities. For each number, I have listed strengths and qualities that will be the most helpful to you in overcoming any obstacles to success and for maximising opportunities.

1 When you are in a park, square or on a beach, assign an area of about 9 metres (30 feet) in diameter in your mind, or mark it with sticks or draw a circle in the sand.

2 Put a few seeds down if you wish, and ask a specific question.

3 If there are more than nine birds, count them and then add the two digits together to give a number between 1 and 9; for example, 17 would equal 8. Count 20 as 2.

4 The number will indicate the approach you should take to a problem or opportunity using the list below.

Now use this list of qualities:

1 **The number of innovation:** leadership, independence, individuality, enthusiasm, drive, assertiveness, mental strength, originality and inspiration.

2 **The number of negotiation:** co-operation, adaptability, consideration of others' points of view, tolerance, balanced opinions and willingness to compromise.

3 **The number of the creative approach:** clear communication, both written and verbal, charisma, persuasiveness, optimism, generosity with time and ideas.

4 **The number of realism:** stability and common sense, practical foundation for ideas, skilled planning, loyalty, trustworthiness, and ability to work within constraints.

5 **The number of voyaging:** expansion of horizons, physical and mental, vision, open-mindedness, eagerness for new knowledge and experiences, versatility.

6 **The number of protectiveness:** altruism, nurturing skills to both those who are close and the world in general, sympathy, idealism, compassion.

7 **The number of wise counsel:** knowledge, respect for tradition, measured thought, spirituality, healing, seeking after truth and harmony.

8 **The number of focus:** self-confidence, focused aims and energy, efficiency and proficiency, competence in any chosen field, logic and analytical powers.

9 The number of crusading: courage, desire for perfection, humanitarianism, integrity, a refusal to be deterred no matter what the obstacle, impassioned speech.

In the next chapter we will look at ways of understanding our pets' needs and feelings on an intuitive level by working with their personal energy fields.

5 | Understanding your pet's aura

I N EARLIER CHAPTERS I have suggested that everything is made up of moving energy. People and animals seem to have unique and relatively constant patterns of energy that inter-mingle and interact with those of other people and animals. It may be that we are attracted to people and pets whose energy patterns are similar to our own or in some way complement our own emotional vibes. Indeed this unseen and intangible connection may partly explain why we are drawn to choose an animal that was not our original planned choice and why we can be attracted by the adoring eyes of a physically unlovely creature (see Chapter 2).

WHAT ARE AURAS?

A name often given to this energy field by those who work in spiritual healing is the aura. Intuitive people may describe this aura in terms of bands of colour. These colours can be matched against traditional colour meanings collected from the spiritual and magical writings of different cultures and ages, and seem to be very accurate in describing the personal-ity and mood of a person or animal around whom they are detected. The colours are sometimes seen in the mind's eye, or to some people they appear as an external halo that is especially visible around the creature or person's head.

EXPLORING AURAS

Like animals, children are very open to hidden powers. Give a young child a box of crayons and before long he or she is scribbling away, perhaps portraying the family cat as purple, or a yellow horse in a field at the back of the house. What they are focusing on are the spiritual rather than physical colours of the creature and usually the colours children use accurately describe the animal's essential nature. The adult conscious mind relies heavily on the actual physiological sight processes and so physically sees only brown or grey fur.

If the idea of auras seems very fanciful, there are many other ways you can understand the hidden aspects of your pet's personality. But before we go any further, let's trick the conscious mind into taking a brief holiday and have a try at working with the subconscious using the concept of colour bands.

1 Begin by looking at any creature you encounter during the day anywhere and say a colour without thinking. You can check the colour against the list on pages 58–66. What you are doing is detecting the current *mood* of the creature. (If you try aura reading more formally, you may find that this colour is much brighter and sparklier than any others you see, and it may change. However, don't try to *see* anything yet.)

2 Now say a second colour straight after. This may reflect the more matt *permanent personality* colour.

3 Do this with creatures you regularly meet and you may find the first colour changes from day to day, but the second is always the same.

4 Try it with your own pet at different times of the day and when different things are happening, such as visitors arriving, before a walk or if the animal is a bit

poorly. By using the list of colours you may find you are
reflecting moods just before they are manifested as
yapping or snappiness.

Seeing auras

You can continue to *interpret* your pet's bands of colour in
this way. But if, as I suspect, you have found the idea useful in
knowing whether your pet needs a cuddle, a walk, to canter or
fly around or to be left alone for a while, then you might like
to have a try at *seeing* auras. I don't mean literally seeing a
physical rainbow around your pets, though a number of very
logical, down-to-earth pet owners do just that. Rather the
picture tends to be in your mind's eye, also known as the
imagination that at times can give us all kinds of inspiration
and tell us things we did not consciously know.

First of all, spend time studying birds flying in the sky,
swooping, taking off and landing again. I have put two bird
tables a little distance apart in my garden and can watch as the
birds weave in and out. What you are looking for is not the individual bird auras, but the silver, grey and blue aural patterns in
your mind's vision or discerned mistily in the sky. In time you
may be able to distinguish the flock leaders by their stronger
shades of colour. Also you could try observing fish darting in
a large, clear pool of water on a sunny day when you may detect
flashes of gold and green. Wild creatures' auras tend to have
bands of colour of similar texture and intensity, though if you
study the same wild creatures regularly you may get more dif-
ferentiated information about individuals (see Chapter 10).

Move next to studying a cat, motionless and totally
relaxed. This time the area around the cat's head or whole
body may seem suffused in purple, a colour often associated
with this most mysterious of domesticated creatures.

After you have spent time colour-watching, you will
probably feel incredibly relaxed. However, you may also discover you have acquired a gift that may in time lead to a career
as an animal healer or pet psychologist. The ability to detect

colours around creatures is very useful in everyday life, as it puts us one step ahead of potential trouble; for example, if a dog goes out spoiling for a fight, his colour would be a harsh, metallic red. The aural colour also suggests when animals are receptive to us introducing changes to their routine, in this case a clear yellow.

As mentioned earlier, you are looking for two main colours when watching your pets, although other colours of the rainbow may be present to a lesser extent. The colour or colours may swirl and follow the contours of the animal or bird as it moves.

The permanent or core aura

This aura is matt and with relatively unbroken colour and can be seen either behind the more transient mood aura (see below) or as the predominant colour when the animal is totally relaxed or asleep. This tells you about the character of the animal and can be seen even in a very young animal. It tends to change only with major events, such as prolonged cruelty or, more positively, giving birth to young, and it may evolve slowly as the animal bonds with its owner(s). You may see it close to the creature's physical body.

Understanding the aura can be a great help when choosing a pet of any age, for if your animal has a clear red aura, for example, he or she will probably remain active and adventurous until old age; a pink aura will indicate patience and gentleness, and a green aura will indicate trustworthiness and devotion. These can be detected in the youngest animal or bird. By noticing if the aura becomes dull or pale you can also become aware that the animal may be feeling chronically unwell or perhaps lacking sufficient contact with nature, which can be a problem for some urban animals.

The mood aura

This aura is more transient, with sparkles, flashes, twinkles and sometimes swirling spirals of colour. It reflects the immediate mood or sometimes a sudden mood change; for example, a flash of orange in a normally docile animal can indicate the need for some time away from children and over-petting. You can use the mood aura to anticipate the best time to give medication (rich brown) or to go for a long walk rather than a short walk, or a gallop rather than a trot if you are observing the aura of a horse (deep blue).

HOW TO SEE AN AURA IN 60 SECONDS

The hardest part about seeing an aura is learning to trust your intuitive or psychic vision. One bonus is that even if you are not aware of seeing colours, the process does make you more able to anticipate pet moods. Maybe the exercise of looking for auras opens intuitive channels in a way that suits you best.

The animal aura usually extends about 6–10 centimetres (2¾–4 inches) around the body. This depends on the spirituality of the animal and not the size of the pet; I have seen a tiny dog with a huge aura bravely defending her owner. As the animal moves, the aura follows the line of the body. At times of excitement or intense protectiveness towards an owner the aura can expand much further and the colours may become momentarily brilliant. When an animal is totally in tune with the owner, the auras of pet and owner merge at the edges. Look at yourself and your pet in the mirror and you may witness this.

The following is a fairly foolproof method for quickly seeing an aura.

1 Start by drawing the outline of the animal or bird whose aura you want to read. Have a set of coloured pencils to hand – you will want at least two shades of each colour, and more if you can find them.

2 Look at the animal framed against a soft light. Wait until he or she is motionless as this is easier for reading the details of an individual aura. In time you will be able to read the aura while an animal moves.

3 Stare hard at your pet. Then close your eyes for a few
seconds, open them, blink and then you will get a vivid
impression of the aura, either externally or in your
mind's vision. Both are as good. The psyche is like a
flashbulb camera and holds the instantaneous image
intact.

4 Record your impressions quickly by scribbling with
coloured pencils around the animal's outline on your
sheet of paper. Use pencils corresponding to the two
main colours you see. As you see the two colours, you
can place the permanent or core aura closest to the
animal's body as a band of colour, and the mood aura as
a more swirling, undulating band, although still
following the outline of the body. On top of the main
colours you can add any other colours, streaks or places
where there is a paler shade or even a space or break in
the aura. The aura may be totally faded – this can
happen with an exhausted or over-stressed creature.

5 You may find it easier to carry out the exercise twice,
the first time to focus on the glittering mood aura and
the second time to focus on the slower moving
permanent aural colour.

6 If you don't see anything at all, try again, but if you are
still unsuccessful do not force it. The ability to see the
aura may emerge when you least expect it.

7 Over the weeks you will begin to *see* the aura at any time
without using any technique.

BUILDING UP THE PICTURE

Study your pet's aura at different times when he or she gets
up, is excited about a walk, hungry or showing hostility or
fear towards another animal. Keep a note of the different
colours you see and what triggers the mood changes. This can
be good for understanding unusual behaviour or can even

explain the onset of a stress-related illness. This can occur in animals and birds just as often as in humans, with tension or anxiety manifested as physical symptoms. You may like to keep a journal in a loose-leaf folder and add the aura images with a note of the date, time and what was happening in the pet's life and the family at the time, as the two are closely linked.

You may find, for example, that the animal's mood aura becomes cloudy whenever someone is smoking in the room. Your pet may be ultra-sensitive to smoke and this may be causing unexplained bad health or temporary bad behaviour. If he or she panics in traffic, you may notice the aura becomes more harshly red when a motorbike is present or when you are near a motorbike, but not a noisy car, bus or van. If you can understand precisely what is upsetting your pet, you can take steps to avoid the negative situation.

Similarly, in an animal from a rescue centre you may find that panic is triggered by something you would not normally consider frightening. One dog I know became acutely distressed when he went near a canal but was not disturbed near to a river or the sea. When Lisa, the owner, enquired at the rescue centre from where she had obtained him, she discovered that he had been thrown in a canal as a puppy, but Lisa had not been told when she first collected the dog, as the records were missing on that day.

Since I first wrote about pet auras I have discovered that they can change two or three minutes before the feared stimulus comes into view, and this can help you to avoid stressful situations; for example, if your dog is distressed by motorbikes you can avoid roads where bikers gather. If the aura becomes red and jagged and the dog becomes distressed, you will know that the dog is not being difficult but that you should change the route or sit in the park for a while until the aura calms and the anticipated danger is past.

The permanent aura is also very useful for understanding your animal: the tiniest dog can be a closet tiger, or your humble moggy can appear surrounded by silver – denoting that he or she is a natural physic – just as we might imagine those sacred cats, who graced the temple of Bastet, the ancient Egyptian cat goddess, may have shone in the full moonlight thousands of years ago (see pages ix–x).

If you see permanent orange around your budgerigar you will know it would like to roam freely. So perhaps he or she can spend more time free-flying around a room or conservatory with the windows closed or perhaps it would benefit from living in a large aviary with other birds. Equally, a powerful stallion may have a gentle brown aura, suggesting that, although he may enjoy sedate canters, he is content in a field eating the daisies and should not be pushed to the limits one might expect from such a powerful creature or entered for horse shows. A tiny Shetland pony may have bright red and blue around her. This would suggest she craves more adventure and a chance to shine; perhaps a horse show away from home occasionally or tiny jumps and a regular child rider would help.

Remember even the tiniest creature, whether tame or wild, has an aura. The following lists the meanings of the colours you see or sense in the aura.

White

Permanent aura: animals with white permanent auras are very special. They possess evolved telepathic and premonitory qualities and the ability to soothe you if you are anxious or afraid, just by their presence. Some people say that these animals have been touched by angels. Certainly you will never regret giving a home to this special friend.

Mood aura: a white mood aura indicates that your animal or bird is suddenly full of the life force and can fill you with hope and energy if you are feeling down. Alternatively, he or she may have detected something or someone good coming into your life.

A very pale, almost invisible white aura can indicate a pet is exhausted or unwell and needs tender, loving care and more rest. There may be something minor, such as a sore paw, which is keeping the animal awake and restless.

Red

Permanent aura: this indicates a very active pet that needs plenty of exercise, space and stimulation whatever its size. Otherwise it may become cranky or irritable. You also have a lion-heart for a companion, no matter how small the animal, so tactfully steer your creature away from confrontations with animals five times its size. You may find, however, that your house rabbit will see off all the neighbouring cats from the garden. Make sure your animal knows you are the boss.

Mood aura: a clear bright-red aura indicates your pet is ready for fun and a walk or a game. Red is also good if you want your pet to mate. A harsh aura may indicate hyperactivity or stress caused by tension, maybe owing to problems with other animals or family arguments. If ignored, this aura can lead to attention-seeking behaviour or to chewing furniture or the pet's own fur or feathers.

A dull, red aura can suggest there is a lot of pent-up energy that needs physical stimulation.

Beware of strange animals with a flashing red aura: they can be aggressive.

Orange

Permanent aura: orange is the colour of a creature of any species that walks alone or would like to. He or she responds to plenty of emotional space and will come to you for patting or petting when it wants attention. Orange does not indicate lack of love but a strong call of the wild; when they do show love, the devotion and altruism of these creatures is boundless.

Mood aura: often seen around small animals such as rabbits or guinea pigs in playschools or children's zoos, orange indicates a wish for time out and a private place to hide. A pale orange seen in the mood auras of rescued animals that have been badly treated shows that the animal has temporarily lost his or her identity. If there is a group of animals or birds that are bullying one of their species, you will see an orange mood aura around the one that is being bullied. Care, a quiet, temporary sanctuary and individual attention will soon improve the situation.

Yellow

Permanent aura: if your pet has a yellow permanent aura, without doubt he or she does not miss a trick and will be waiting at the door or the food bowl before you have taken your coat off at night or surfaced from sleep in the morning. A pet with this aura is an excellent companion that always knows the way home even if you don't. If it is a cat, he or she will catch any mice within half a mile of the house, and knows the going rate in pet treats for such endeavours.

Mood aura: when your pet displays a yellow mood aura this is a good time to try the psychic games I listed on pages 24–8, as he or she is totally alert and eager to try new activities. Yellow is also useful when training animals or changing bad habits, even in older animals.

If your cat has been missing from home a lot recently and it has a dull yellow aura, this can indicate that it may have found a more comfortable billet in another house along the road. Dull yellow also appears when a new family member, whether a boy- or girlfriend, baby or new animal, is first introduced to the household and your pet feels natural resentment, even if the pet is seemingly friendly to the 'intruder'; extra attention to the resident animal usually clears this up.

Green

Permanent aura: green is a colour of pure love and fidelity that will deepen over the years. This pet really would offer its life for you. A pet with a green permanent aura is a gentle loving companion that will sit by you for hours if you are sad or lonely and will listen to your woes and share the good times equally.

Fish sometimes have streaks of green in their auras and if you have a sensitive breed, such as koi carp, this may increase as you get to know the individual fish.

Pale green may indicate an animal that feels neglected, although this may be unjustified. It is common in rescued animals and may also appear if you have been working extra-long hours away from home or have been distracted by numerous demands on your time and have cut down on your contact with the animal to feeding and hurried walks. In both cases, extra affection and reassurance will restore the natural grass-green. You can trust this animal with children, smaller creatures and vulnerable people.

Mood aura: you know your animal is feeling happy and loving being with you when it displays a green mood aura. You may notice a rich green aura while grooming a rabbit or exercising a horse. It is a sign of pure contentment and harmony with you. If you looked in a mirror you would probably detect your own matching aura. It is good for attempting telepathic communication.

Blue

Permanent aura: blue is seen in very altruistic, noble-spirited animals; you may be surprised to observe deep blue around the scruffiest pooch. These are the animals most likely to be the heroes or heroines of dramatic rescues or that are highly intelligent and able to perform complex tasks for severely disabled or chronically sick owners, or to anticipate the onset of an illness.

Look for a blue permanent aura when you choose a pet, even as a baby, for this will always be a loyal friend that would love you and share hardship or misfortune without complaint.

Birds have blue in their auras to reflect the sky and you may notice it when a bird you own is in free flight.

Mood aura: this aura shows that your pet has healing and harmony to offer you, usually at a time when you are stressed or suffering overload. Spend time with the animal alone, whether on a long walk or sitting quietly at the fireside, and you will experience a flow of healing energy and spiritual as well as emotional unity.

Purple

Permanent aura: a purple permanent aura is most often seen around those mystical creatures – cats. Whether a pedigree Persian or a common or garden tabby, your cat really is an old soul, even if reincarnation theories are not for you. Any creature with this aura can lead you towards a more balanced way of life where activity comes in concentrated bursts (catch that mouse and then back to sleep).

Animals with a purple permanent aura are an excellent antidote to a frantic lifestyle and will calm down hyperactive children and adults. Any animal or bird with a purple aura is incredibly psychic and – be warned – an excellent mind-reader that will disappear an hour before even the most secretly arranged veterinary appointment.

Mood aura: purple is another good aura for pet owners to absorb. If your cat or any other animal has deep silvery purple round him or her, slow down and look through half-closed eyes (this is good feline etiquette) and share your animal's world view for a while; this is beneficial for sorting out your own priorities.

Pink

Permanent aura: look for a pink permanent aura when choosing a pet if there are children around, as this creature will guard and guide your offspring. Always patient, kind and unselfish, the pure pink aura promises unconditional love and loyalty and forgiveness of human frailty.

Even with creatures that have been abused or neglected

there may still be a pale pink glow, because deep down animals are trusting, and if you have the patience you will see the deep pink return.

Mood aura: like green, pink is linked to love and affection and may appear around an animal or bird when you are petting it, or when you are touching any animal or bird or sharing quiet activities or relaxation together. However, you may also detect it if you are feeling lonely and unloved or just plain cranky. Your pet is sending you waves of love and a vote of confidence, so bask in it and accept what a good judge of character your pet is.

Brown

Permanent aura: this is the rich golden brown of a newly ploughed field or of autumn leaves and is mostly seen around horses, dogs that work in the rescue services or any animals that spend a great deal of time outdoors. Brown indicates unquestioning loyalty and a fierce protectiveness not only to owners but also to anyone in need. No matter how dark the night or long the road, this creature will be there to encourage you.

A dull brown aura, especially in an elderly animal, means that he or she needs a sanctuary of quiet in the home and extra attention paid to its health to boost its energy levels.

Mood aura: a brown mood aura indicates total acceptance of whatever your plans may be. However, pale brown in a dog suggests that a long walk in the park or local nature reserve or a day in the country or on the seashore would be especially welcome, especially if it is an urban animal; for a horse, a long canter along a wild bridle path will restore its normal golden hue.

Grey

Permanent aura: a creature with a grey permanent aura is a creature of the night that needs plenty of walks in the dark, and a dark corner in its cage or a secret cupboard as a refuge at home. This creature lives with you because he or she has chosen to and so a grey pet is a great honour and gift. They tend to make their own private place, which must be respected, or they may go missing occasionally; however, they will always return looking triumphant.

Mood aura: your animal may be feeling out of sorts, confused and temporarily difficult or withdrawn. Let your pet sort out his or her angst; it is not usually human-related, but will be the call of the wild or a hormonal downswing. With exotic pets that display this mood colour regularly, make their environment similar to their indigenous conditions, even if they are home bred. More sand, plants and rocks for snakes and lizards, for example, and maybe a mini-pool will make them a lot happier.

Black

Permanent aura: this may be seen in very old or sick animals that are gradually letting go of life, in animals that are grieving for a family member who has moved away, or in rescued animals that have been very badly treated and have drawn a veil over their feelings. With kindness and care it will lift, but as this pet will need a great deal of emotional input, a creature with a black permanent aura is not one to choose if you have children or a busy work life and frequent absences because of work. The animal is often best off with one owner.

Mood aura: black is rarely seen in pets as a blanket colour, as animals are usually optimistic. However, the regular appearance of black streaks in the aura can be an early warning system. They may suggest that the creature's lifestyle needs readjusting; more exercise for an overweight pet or quiet for a highly strung one will help to relieve the situation before the condition manifests itself as a physical problem. Also, watch out for secret bullying by other animals or teasing by humans. In a chronically sick animal, you may need to change its medication or try alternative treatment, whether conventional or holistic.

Silver

Permanent aura: you really did hit the jackpot with this pet. Animals with a silver permanent aura are, like those with purple, the natural psychics and healers of the animal kingdom. They are always one step ahead of you, anticipating your moods and fetching your slippers or waiting at the door almost before you had thought of going out alone. This pet's warnings should be taken seriously, and if he or she does not like a stranger, be cautious. Silver is also seen around birds that soar high in the sky, especially hawks or larks, as it is a colour of freedom and the high sky.

Mood aura: you can be sure that your silver pet is picking up on something beyond your senses. If the animal is happy and calm then it may be an angelic presence or friendly deceased great-grandmother who has popped in to check on your well-being (you may even smell her perfume). However, if the dog becomes agitated or growls you should temporarily move away from the place or person, because the animal has detected unfriendly energy, whether normal or paranormal, or a person who has hidden malice.

If you see harsh silver streaks in an otherwise tranquil aura when the animal is in a particular spot in your house and is unable to settle there, you may have a patch of negative earth energies. These may be caused by electrical pollution, such as a nearby mobile-phone mast, or some sorrow on the land that occurred centuries before and has concentrated in that spot. Simply place an amethyst geode (the tiny crystals embedded in rock) on a small table over the spot and the problem will clear. Wash the amethyst frequently.

Gold

Permanent aura: if you watch pet hero of the year ceremonies on a colour television set, you will see this incredibly rare aura as well as a rich blue glinting around the award winners' heads. Such a pet is to be treasured, though you may feel it is not truly yours but belongs to a higher order. If angels took animal form this would be one. A pet with a gold permanent aura is a wise helper and one that will always bring out the greatest good in you.

Mood aura: a gold mood aura is seen in those rare moments when you gallop along a beach at dawn on a horse with the wind blowing its mane, or when a dog dives into a pile of leaves or emerges glittering from the sunlit sea, or your cage bird sings joyously from the tallest palm in your conservatory, or your garden rabbit tunnels under its run and makes its first burrow. Try to make time for those special moments so that you can share your creature's experience, moving for a moment or two beyond the mundane world.

IMPROVING YOUR PET'S AURA

If your pet's permanent aura seems clouded or too harsh there are various methods you can use to infuse your animal gradually with positive energies. Crystals are a gentle but effective way of filling an animal's aura with calm or energy and restoring well-being. You can place crystals beneath a pet bed or leave one in water for eight hours to infuse the water with its energies, or you can hang one in a birdcage or small animal pen.

You can use a crystal that is the same colour as the creature's pale or dull aura, but choose one that has a brighter, more vibrant hue. This will restore the creature's own healing and health-maintenance system. In the same way a muted, gentle crystal shade will soften a harsh aura colour that may be reflected in hyperactive or snappy behaviour in an animal. You should see the mood aura lighten or brighten instantly, although it may take up to a week of daily use for a permanent aura that is tired or overactive to respond to the crystal's full beneficial effects.

If an animal is naturally timid you can use a red stone for a period of weeks or months to introduce the colour of courage into its aura. If your pet is constantly hyperactive or disobedient, a soft-pink rose quartz or green jade will be beneficial.

The following crystals are useful for strengthening or improving an aura:

Agates

Use opaque, banded agates in muted pinks, oranges and brown; if a pet that lives in the centre of a town develops a very harsh aura or one streaked with black, this will be due to the effects of noise and pollution.

Amber

A golden orange organic gem of great antiquity, often containing fossilised plants or insects, amber will gently energise a dull or lifeless aura after a pet has been ill or become exhausted with nursing young or after there has been some stress in the family. Amber is helpful for older animals that are no longer very mobile, and for all lizards, insects and snakes.

Aquamarine

Use a tiny crystal, light blue or blue-green, to restore health to the aura after an animal has suffered a shock, or after an accident or if another animal has attacked it. Place an aquamarine in a fish tank or pond to keep the fishes' auras healthy and to counter pollution for fish that are kept in towns.

Jade

A harsh aura of any colour will be softened by jade, which will slow hyperactivity or destructive behaviour in pets caused by frustration or an imbalance in the creature's system. It will also lighten the aura of an animal that has been ill-treated or badly frightened.

Jasper

Red, orange and yellow jasper are all excellent crystals for strengthening a weak or almost non-existent aura in an old or exhausted pet. Orange is especially good for empowering the auras of horses and larger animals or those that have been bullied by siblings or others of the species.

Moss agate

This stone can be green and blue or a colourless, translucent stone with green inclusions. Moss agate will help to keep healthy the auras of all urban animals or those that spend a lot of time indoors, by reconnecting them with nature. Also, use moss agate for restoring the health of any creature's aura after an operation or long illness. It is also helpful for all naturally burrowing creatures, such as hamsters (they make huge piles of bedding in their cages to replicate their natural burrows in the desert).

Rose quartz

This will strengthen the aura of a nursing mother or any animal that has been neglected before coming into your home. It will also soothe over-bright colours in the aura of a hyperactive animal or one that has become snappy or aggressive because of teasing or attack by another creature.

Turquoise

Use a blue-green turquoise to cast protection around the aura of any pet, especially if there are hostile neighbours or fast roads where the animal lives. This is also a useful stone for keeping the auras of birds and small animals healthy and balanced, especially those that live in cages or hutches.

ANIMAL SPEAK

Some pet owners believe that if we talk to our animals they will reply telepathically and our minds can interpret their feelings as words. A number of successful pet healers around the world have used this method to diagnose what is wrong with an animal, and found it especially useful for diagnosing stress-related illnesses (see pages 96–7). One explanation for this ability to interpret animal thoughts as words could be that the aura of the animal and the owner temporarily merge so the two minds become as one. I have also seen this explanation given for human telepathy.

Certainly, if you want to get into the mind of your animal, whether to share a deep level of communication or to understand a health problem that is eluding conventional diagnosis and treatment, one effective method is by momentarily moving your mind into the aura of the animal. This is also a way you can give healing to your pet. This merging of consciousness may also be the way some animals are able to recognise danger or the onset of illness in a sleeping owner, and there are examples of this in the chapters of this book (see pages 23 and 35).

PRACTISING AURA MERGING

The secret of horse and dog whisperers is that they speak continuously in a soft, mesmeric tone that puts the animal and themselves into a light trance state so that the barriers between the energy fields melt. We have a number of tones of voice we use to our pets: affectionate, light-hearted, soothing and occasionally cross. But this 'animal speak' is closer to a chant and can be used for all forms of telepathic communication and suggestion. It is useful when you want to modify an animal's behaviour or trigger self-healing in your pet and reawaken its sluggish immune system. You might like to try this method when you and the animal are relaxed.

Create a time of stillness when you sit by the pet and share a communal quiet space in which communication through aura merging can take place. Evenings when the house is quiet are perfect; make sure there are no outside distractions. If working with a horse, twilight is a good time, when your horse is resting in its stable. In this case make physical contact by touching the horse lightly as you work.

1 Face the animal (but do not make eye contact with a cat, as they tend to dislike this).

2 Begin with a simple message of love spoken aloud, but softly and repetitively, over and over for a minute or so; for example, 'You are a beautiful cat/rabbit/canary.'

3 Let the words get softer until they become a whisper and then fade into silence.

4 Wait for about a minute and then repeat the message.

5 Do this three or four times.

6 As you speak, visualise the animal's aura moving closer so that similar colours from your aura and the animal's flow in both directions and enclose you both in a swirling mist. These are usually green, pink, purple and blue. If you find it hard to picture the colours, use a fibre-optic lamp to simulate the experience until your own psyche takes over.

7 After the third or fourth time you may feel a stirring in your mind as though light waves or a ripple of leaves were moving between you and your pet in bands of green or pink light. At this point you will be communicating heart to heart with the animal or bird.

8 Let the colours fade and separate, and then repeat the experience a day or so later. This time you may hear words in the silence; these would be the creature's thoughts translated by your unconscious mind into what is often a soft, low voice, or you may receive one or two distinct images straight from the animal's mind.

9 You can use this method to ask your pet what is wrong, to send healing (see page 99) or to receive information about any aspect of the pet's feelings and to share your own.

As you become more practised you will only need to look at your pet through half-closed eyes to see the aural colours merging. If your pet has a message for you, he or she might sit silently and still, looking at you expectantly. Ask softly, 'What is it you wish to tell me?' Take any warnings or advice seriously, because, as we have seen, animal instincts are so much more evolved psychically and in tune with unseen influences than our own.

In the next chapter we will look more into the hidden personality of pets and consider if and how their birth dates, the movement of the Moon and the seasons might affect their mood and behaviour.

6 | Astrology and pets

EVEN RELATIVELY SCEPTICAL PEOPLE take at least a passing interest in their daily horoscope. Astrology seems to be able to describe a person's character, strengths and weaknesses and also his or her potential. Perhaps, then, it is unsurprising that pet astrology is becoming popular among pet owners who are eager to understand more about their pets' personalities. Through astrology it may be possible to predict a puppy's, kitten's or foal's needs, foibles and compatibility with a prospective owner or the creatures with whom it will share a home or pen, by using its birth date and time of birth to find the relevant Sun sign. Some people even take birth signs into account for breeding purposes.

However, I would not necessarily recommend that you get a full pet horoscope, as animals and birds are relatively straightforward creatures; a birth date provides a good enough general template for the different types of personality.

DISCOVERING A PET'S STAR SIGN

Pedigree animals' Sun or zodiac signs are especially easy to identify because these pets come complete with a certificate giving the date and maybe even the time of birth. However, you can usually find out when any puppy, kitten, foal, young bird or small animal was born by asking the person from whom you obtained it, who will probably have the day etched in their heart because of a sleepless night or huge vet bill associated with the event. Alternatively you can examine early inoculation records, as these are given at set ages, from which you could roughly work out a birth date.

With rescued animals or creatures you obtain later in their life, there may be no birth date so you have to work another way. Choose an animal that feels compatible with you by reading the aura or using one of the other methods I suggested on pages 10–15 or your own preferences; when you know the creature better you can deduce its birth sign from its characteristics and, as a result, be more able to anticipate its moods and needs. You can even detect the birth date of certain fish; I have an Arian goldfish who, right from the start, leaped up for food and bullied the other fish so that he was always first in line. The breeder told me the fish was about six weeks old when I bought him and I worked back from that date, which meant that he was born at the end of March; coupled with his assertive character, I am certain the fish's star sign is mid-Aries.

PET SUN SIGNS

♈ Aries, the Ram (21 March–20 April):

Pets born under Aries are free spirits, totally without guile, independent (unless they want fussing), energetic, competitive (they make good show animals) and very determined to get or go their own way. Although natural leaders of any other animals in the home, they will be very loyal to their owners. They are fearless in protecting those they love. Keep them stimulated and establish boundaries. They are better with adults than children.

♉ Taurus, the Bull (21 April–21 May):

Taurus pets are patient, reliable, practical, loyal and home-loving.

They demand the most comfortable spot in the house or stabling, the choicest brand of food and a lot of grooming and attention. Indeed they can become very possessive about what is theirs, even uneaten cat food – woe betide any stray who attempts to make off with their leftovers!

Tauruses are incredibly attached to their owners and their homes and thrive on a regular routine. Watch their tendency towards overweight and their disinclination to exercise. They are tolerant with children and young animals and also make a good pet for older people.

♊ Gemini, the Heavenly Twins (22 May–21 June):

The most intelligent of zodiacal signs, Gemini pets are very vocal and love new challenges and adventures; they are natural clowns and crave attention. Although physically they may seem rather stand-offish, they will often sit or stand close to you. They are constantly on the move, and even older animals will remain playful. Gemini pets need a great deal of exercise or stimulation and are ideal with teenagers and with anyone with an active or sporting lifestyle.

♋ Cancer, the Crab (22 June–22 July):

Cancer pets are naturally home-loving, and, whether male or female, are the nurturers of the pet world, taking care of smaller or weaker animals, babies, children and, most of all, their owners. They are extremely sensitive and intuitive and will anticipate your mood before you are aware of it. On the whole they do not enjoy holidays away from home or unfamiliar territory and are better left with a sitter; it is best not to use kennels or a cattery. They are happiest with owners who spend a great deal of time at home.

♌ Leo, the Lion (23 July–23 August):

Leos are the noblest of pets, even if they are a mongrel or a mixed-breed cat or horse, and are constantly grooming themselves. They love nothing better than competitions. As long as they are the leader, they will be kind to other animals. Leos are among the most altruistic of pets and would lay down their lives to save their owners' or anyone in need. Because they need a lot of attention and praise, they are best with one owner, as they sometimes find it hard to share his or her affection, even with another human.

♍ Virgo, the Maiden (24 August–22 September):

Perfect – or purrfect – in every way, your Virgo cat will always be glossy and well groomed and would be ideal in a well-furnished home as Virgo cats rarely scratch or shred. Virgo animals of all kinds will be good show pets, winning the best-of-breed or half-breed awards. They are also happy to be left alone while their owner is at work. They can, however, be highly strung and may panic or become ill if stressed or if there is too much noise or confusion. Virgo rabbits are good house pets as they are readily trained.

♎ Libra, the Scales (23 September–23 October):

Libras are very charismatic pets and enjoy petting, patting and admiration from others – the more the merrier. They are even-tempered creatures, slow to be provoked by other animals or children and generally sunny, but are very changeable in their food preferences and are faddy eaters. They are also incredibly lazy animals and would snooze their life away. Libras are good if you want a pet companion that is popular with everyone, and they make good urban pets.

♏ Scorpio, the Scorpion (24 October–22 November):

Scorpio is a very psychic pet that you may feel you can never fully fathom. You need to earn this creature's trust. Once you gain it he or she would walk through fire for you. Equally, Scorpios will never forget the visitor who kicked or ignored them. The squirrels of the pet world, Scorpios will forever bury or hide objects and they are also natural hunters, so a Scorpio cat will be excellent if you have problems with rodents. However, Scorpios are incredibly stubborn and can be drama kings or queens if they feel neglected or unfairly shouted at. They are good for people who enjoy a slightly unpredictable pet.

♐ Sagittarius, the Archer (23 November–21 December):
These are the noisiest and most active pets in the zodiac; they may suddenly go missing for a few hours or days. They love company – the larger the household the better – and a varied routine. Good with strangers and in unfamiliar places, Sagittarians will not usually panic in crowds or while travelling. They are very good at learning new things and are excellent performers, if they feel in the right mood. However, they may lack the staying power for animal obedience classes or horse shows, and so on. Sagittarians are best in a very active household; they especially enjoy the company of men and teenage boys.

♑ Capricorn, the Goat (22 December–20 January):
This is the pet that needs the least maintenance of all the zodiac signs. The Capricorn animal is totally reliable and will never beg for titbits or complain about going out on wet nights or eating economy food. They are very stable pets and so are good with visiting children, although they can sometimes find toddlers irritating and will tend to retreat to their private place if they are around. Loyal from the earliest days, Capricorns will never be lured away or turn their back on you whatever your troubles may be. They are cautious to the point of obsession, and prefer older or quieter people rather than partygoers or a large family.

♒ Aquarius, the Water Carrier (21 January–18 February):
Aquarians only really need owners for their basic requirements; nevertheless, they make excellent pets. They are totally unconcerned about what you can give them materially and are good companions on life's road, with their endearing and often quirky behaviour and total honesty. They need a great deal of freedom and time to be alone, and so Aquarians are ideal if you are out a great deal. They are curious and intelligent and will explore their own territory and the world beyond, if they are given the opportunity. Aquarians are not particularly good with other animals; they can bark or yowl if upset. However, they are wonderful as a solo pet, especially for

a couple who will not make constant emotional demands on their companion creature.

)(Pisces, the Fish (19 February–20 March):

Pisces is another very intuitive, home-loving creature whose world is bound up with that of the owner. Your Pisces pet will share your moods and so will be a very comforting pet when you are feeling lonely or unloved. Pisces pets are very dreamy and will often stare out of the window or into space for hours on end. Although good with babies and children as well as sick and unhappy people, the Pisces pet can be prone to depression and to psychosomatic or stress-related illnesses and can react badly to family quarrels, smoke and physical pollution. Pisces will grieve dreadfully if an animal or person within the family is hospitalised, leaves home or has died. They are especially good as a woman or girl's pet.

ASTROLOGICAL COMPATIBILITY

The animal–owner and animal–animal compatibility within a household, aviary or animal pen is no different from that of human lovers or partners. Although you may decide to choose a pet that is totally compatible with your own birth sign, different factors will emerge in interactions with other household members and pets. You might find it interesting to watch how a pet or human with a less instantly compatible astrological sign learns to give houseroom to others in the household and form an exciting mix.

Sign	Compatible, instantly easy and has harmonious relationships with:	Less harmonious, but able to balance the other's good and bad qualities with a refreshingly different worldview with:	Can have initial personality clashes, but is stimulating company and can teach you a lot about tolerance and your own blind spots, if you are:
Aries	Aries, Taurus, Gemini, Leo, Sagittarius, Aquarius, Pisces	Cancer, Libra its opposing sign, Capricorn	Virgo, Scorpio
Taurus	Taurus, Gemini, Cancer, Virgo, Capricorn, Pisces, Aries	Leo, Scorpio its opposing sign, Aquarius	Libra, Sagittarius
Gemini	Gemini, Cancer, Leo, Libra, Aquarius, Aries, Taurus	Virgo, Sagittarius its opposing sign, Pisces	Scorpio, Capricorn
Cancer	Cancer, Leo, Virgo, Scorpio, Pisces, Taurus, Gemini	Libra, Capricorn its opposing sign, Aries	Sagittarius, Aquarius
Leo	Leo, Virgo, Libra, Sagittarius, Aries, Gemini, Cancer	Scorpio, Aquarius its opposing sign, Taurus	Capricorn, Pisces

Virgo	Virgo, Libra, Scorpio, Capricorn, Taurus, Cancer, Leo	Sagittarius, Pisces its opposing sign, Gemini	Aquarius, Aries
Libra	Libra, Scorpio, Sagittarius, Aquarius, Gemini, Leo, Virgo	Capricorn, Aries its opposing sign, Cancer	Pisces, Taurus
Scorpio	Scorpio, Sagittarius, Capricorn, Pisces, Cancer, Virgo, Libra	Aquarius, Taurus its opposing sign, Leo	Aries, Gemini
Sagittarius	Sagittarius, Capricorn, Aquarius, Aries, Leo, Libra, Scorpio	Pisces, Gemini its opposing sign, Virgo	Taurus, Cancer
Capricorn	Capricorn, Aquarius, Pisces, Taurus, Virgo, Scorpio, Sagittarius	Aries, Cancer its opposing sign, Libra	Gemini, Leo
Aquarius	Aquarius, Pisces and Aries, Gemini, Libra, Sagittarius, Capricorn	Taurus, Leo its opposing sign, Scorpio	Cancer, Virgo
Pisces	Pisces, Aries, Taurus, Cancer, Scorpio, Capricorn, Aquarius	Gemini, Virgo its opposing sign, Sagittarius	Leo, Libra

PETS AND THE MOON

As creatures of nature, animals, birds and reptiles are possibly more strongly influenced than humans by the different monthly phases of the Moon and the individual Sun signs through which the Moon passes during each month. By understanding the cumulative effect of earth and cosmic energies, to which even the most urban pet is subject, you can anticipate when your pet may be feeling restless or especially co-operative and modify his or her routine accordingly.

YOUR PET AND THE MOON PHASES

Medieval woodcuts often portray dogs howling to the full Moon, and this is an image that appears on most Tarot cards of the Moon. Animals are especially sensitive to the subtle shift in cosmic energies that occur within every month as the Moon waxes (or increases), reaches full Moon and thereafter wanes (decreases). If you understand these interim lunar energy changes you can anticipate a pet's needs and understand or counteract any moodiness or crankiness it may exhibit. Indeed you may find that as you focus on these lunar energies they explain some of your own seemingly irrational feelings at certain times in the month. Although this applies whether you are a man or woman, women and female animals do seem more strongly affected than their male counterparts.

You can find out the current Moon phase at any time by looking in the sky if the weather is clear, or by consulting the weather page in a newspaper, an almanac – such as *Old Moore's Almanac* – or a diary that gives Moon phases for each day. There are eight astronomical phases of the Moon, but energy-wise you can work with three broader energy bands: waxing, full and waning. During the waxing (or increasing) energy phase the light of the Moon increases in size from right to left (a crescent Moon is seen on the right and points left). You may see the waxing Moon in the sky during the day.

You can count this phase from when you see the crescent Moon in the sky until the night of the full Moon.

After the night of the full Moon, which appears in the sky around sunset, the light and energies decrease also from right to left. The final crescent on the left that points right then disappears, marking the end of the waning phase. As the Moon wanes so it rises later until it is most clearly seen in the early morning of the following day. About two and a half days later the crescent appears on the right again.

If you want to be a real purist, remember that the Moon is full for only the second it rises, and thereafter it wanes. But in practice, full Moon energies are from moonrise to set and its energies are manifested in animal and human lives for two days either side of each full Moon appearance.

THE WAXING MOON AND PETS

Even normally sedate animals and birds may become more frisky, energetic and curious as the waxing phase progresses. It is a good time for training animals into positive habits, for gradually making changes in their routine, for introducing new animals or family members to the household and for taking your pet on trips away from home or to unfamiliar territory. It is also the right time to take your pet on any necessary veterinary visits or for starting medication while the animal is cheerful and mentally receptive.

THE FULL MOON AND PETS

Especially intuitive animals and birds are aware of this most powerful phase a day or two in advance. This is the time when cosmic energies are at full power but also a time of instability, as astrologically the Moon is in opposition – or the opposite side of the sky – to the Sun. Since the animal will have picked up the powerful energies of change, you might as well ride the wave as be submerged by it. Therefore, it is a good time for the animal to make any major changes, such as moving house, undergoing a necessary operation, being taken to stud, artificial insemination of a female or for introducing a breeding animal to a new mate. It is also a suitable time for an animal to attend shows or races, as success vibes are high during a full Moon.

Make sure your pet has the opportunity for physical exercise. He or she may benefit from new toys or routes for walks, or a different area around which it can fly or run freely; even a hamster will benefit from a different arrangement of tunnels to play in. Also make sure your pet has plenty of attention, and is especially well nourished and rested. Avoid taking him or her near to strange animals except for breeding or competitive purposes, as fights may break out at this time.

THE WANING MOON AND PETS

This extends from the day after the full Moon until the waning crescent disappears from the sky. Your pet may be more irritable during this period; it may tire easily but seem unable to relax. Try to introduce quiet activities, such as gentle walks and massages, and add soothing flower essences (see pages 165–9) to the pet water. Keep to routines wherever possible and prepare a dark, quiet place for your pet, as even a normally gregarious animal may need to find a retreat.

Watch out for potential hazards, such as illness, as the pet's protective radar is at its weakest at this time. Resistance to germs is lower than usual during this period, especially on the very last days of the Moon's cycle. Also, a pet is more vulnerable to losing its way towards the end of the Moon's cycle. However, this time is also a good period to get rid of any bad habits your pet may have and to start it on a new diet.

THE ZODIAC AND THE MOON

The Moon travels around the Earth every 29½ days. In its orbit it passes through each of the Sun or zodiac signs, for about two and a half days. Although this is not as significant as the broader Moon phases, the sensitive animal seems to pick up the prevailing energies of each Sun sign as the Moon passes through it, and the Moon will amplify the effects of the energies of that sign. The effect is most pronounced when the Moon is in the pet's own birth sign each month.

If an animal is behaving oddly, check the Sun sign through which the Moon is currently passing; you will find this information in the horoscope sections of national and local newspapers and also in diaries. You may like to keep your own Moon behaviour pattern chart for your pet(s) for the transitional periods and the broader Moon phases. Before long you may see a pattern emerging, which with a minor adjustment to the pet's routine can keep it harmonious throughout the month.

Moon in Aries

This is a time when an animal may be restless and unable to settle, even when introduced to new activities or stimuli. Focus on short bursts of exercise or games. Watch your pet carefully, as even a stable pet might take risks or start fights. This is an excellent time for taking animals to stud.

Moon in Taurus

When the Moon is in Taurus it is a very relaxed period for animals; even urban pets will be tuned to the earth and enjoy time outdoors. Females on heat will be very fertile and have strong, healthy babies. The animal will also be especially patient, so take the opportunity to carry out unpopular forms of grooming or to administer general medication. I change flea collars, which my cats hate, in this Moon period.

Moon in Gemini

This is a very unstable period, so keep everything calm and in routine for a pet. Yowlers yowl and howlers howl more than usual at this time. However, a pet will be open to communication of all kinds now, so you may feel especially in tune with your animal's feelings and needs.

Moon in Cancer

When the Moon is in Cancer it is another favoured time for domestic harmony with your pet, although he or she may become intensely secretive, hiding objects and even him or herself. It is a good time for bonding with new animals or new family members in the home. However, pets are also incredibly sensitive to affronts so be soft-toned and tactful to avoid tantrums.

Moon in Leo

If you have a chance to show your pet or to enter it into competitions, this is the time for success. If not you may need to give extra attention to your pet, perhaps giving a dog a new collar, for example. Inviting visitors into the home or going for extra walks where your pet will be fussed and admired would also be beneficial at this time.

Moon in Virgo

When the Moon is in Virgo it is probably the best time for washing bedding and spring-cleaning a pet's hutch in addition to its usual daily care. However, it is definitely not the right time for major routine alterations. Any health or healing work could be undertaken now, as the pet will be especially receptive to any therapeutic work.

Moon in Libra

Here is another good time for breeding or for introducing breeding partners or indeed any new animals or family members to your pet. Generally the animal will be feeling very harmonious, though you may notice a favourite food is suddenly rejected as the desire for alternatives kicks in (you could take this opportunity to be sneaky and introduce a cheaper brand).

Moon in Scorpio

You could set your pet up in a fortune-telling booth when the Moon is in Scorpio, as he or she will be incredibly psychic and tuned in to you. However, likes and dislikes may temporarily become more intense, so avoid any unnecessary areas of conflict, routine visits to the vet or the grooming parlour. It is another good time for breeding.

Moon in Sagittarius

Your normally home-loving pet may get the urge for adventure, so if you do not want him or her wandering or running off, provide novelty and extra exercise within a controlled environment. This is not the right time to let a dog off the leash in unfamiliar territory, as the hunting instincts may kick in. Neither is it recommended to move animals to new homes, as they may go looking for their old ones. However, it is good for new routines and learning new behaviour patterns or tricks, but only practise in short bursts, as your pet's attention span will be limited in this Moon time.

Moon in Capricorn

All animals become more cautious when the Moon is in Capricorn, and so this is a time when they prefer to be in familiar places with familiar people. Even boisterous animals will be quieter and more settled. However, guard against signs that your pet is depressed or feeling unwanted, especially if there are new animals or people around.

Moon in Aquarius

If a normally conservative animal starts behaving oddly when the Moon is in Aquarius, do not send for the pet psychologist.

This Moon time will have animals chasing their tails, walking backwards and drinking the fish water. Tolerance is the best policy; there are only two and a half days before normality returns. Animals may also not want to be patted or fussed, so allow extra space for them.

Moon in Pisces

'Treading on eggshells' is the phrase to sum up this time, for most animals and birds will react adversely to sudden noises, crowded places and family quarrels. Pets are super-psychic as well and so they may pick up your mood changes almost before you are aware of them yourself. Gentle words and a slow routine will make this a harmonious phase.

SEASONAL ENERGIES AND PETS

Wild animals are very tuned in to the seasonal energies. The movement of the herds and the fish, bird migration, and animal hibernation and breeding are triggered not only by temperature changes but also by alterations in the patterns of light and darkness as well as more subtle earth energies that indicate that winter or spring is approaching. They know by natural instinct when it is time to store berries and nuts for the winter or to begin seeking a suitable mate. Domesticated animals, however, have become more in harmony with the rhythms of their owners than with the seasons. With the advent of 24-hour heating and lighting we have moved far from the days when people rested more during the long winter nights and then worked in the fields in the longer summer days. However, domestic animals do still respond to the call of the seasons, even if they live 20 floors up in a centrally heated apartment block. If we can recognise these seasonal changes, we can help them to live in harmony with their innate body rhythms. We will also understand why the rabbit leaps around the garden on the first day of spring and the cat makes a den in a dark cupboard in late autumn, even though she never ventures further than the litter tray outside the back door summer or winter.

The four main seasons of the year are marked by the three-monthly divisions of the astronomical equinoxes and solstices. In the southern hemisphere the seasons move round by six months, so that in Australia, for example, the height of summer comes in mid-December rather than mid-June; this is marked by the midsummer solstice or longest day when solar influences are at their greatest.

Because the solstices and equinoxes are astronomical markers, the dates may vary by a day or two depending on the movement in the skies, but animals and birds pick up the changing seasonal energies at least a week beforehand. The most intense effects are manifest around the actual solstice or equinox. Even animals in countries where there are only two seasons seem to respond to these astronomical markers, especially if their distant ancestors came from the more temperate northern climes.

Spring

21 March–20 June (for the northern hemisphere), from the spring equinox to the summer solstice

The vernal equinox or spring equinox, 21–23 March, marks the transition point between the dark and light halves of the year. At the spring equinox, the Sun rises due east and sets due west, giving exactly twelve hours of daylight.

Long before the days of intensive farming methods, which have disrupted the natural cycles, the spring equinox marked the time when hens began to lay eggs again after the winter, hence the origin of Easter eggs (in pre-Christian times these were given as a tribute to Ostara, the Viking Goddess of Spring). The mad March hare, another symbol of Easter, was the sacred animal of Ostara, and was often noticed bounding around in the warmer weather around Easter time.

This is the time when all creatures, even the laziest pets, start paper shredding and nest building. As their thoughts turn to mating, they will make advances towards any of the opposite sex of their species they encounter, and even neutered tomcats serenade the world from the rooftops. Animals and birds are full of energy and enthusiasm for new experiences. They are playful and eager to be sniffing and digging outdoors, even when it is raining and chilly.

If your animal cannot breed, give him or her soft toys and material to make a nest as well as opportunities to explore new territory. Young animals will be made welcome by older female animals and birds, but males may be more aggressive to one another even in a normally tranquil household (you may notice this among humans as well as pets).

Summer

21 June–20 September (for the northern hemisphere), from the summer solstice to the autumn equinox

The summer solstice – around 20–22 June – marks the high point of the year, the longest day, and is the peak of the Sun's light and power. Animals and birds will be strutting and preening, and fish will be leaping in the sunlight. This is the peak time of energy and strength when an animal or bird is at its most outgoing and competitive. The long days mean pets will sleep less and need more vigorous exercise and opportunities to roam freely and connect with nature, even though the nights will now grow imperceptibly longer from this point.

Share the joys of the summer with your pet and be outdoors whenever possible with them, even if it has been a disappointing summer weather-wise.

Autumn

21 September–21 December (for the northern hemisphere), from the autumn equinox to the midwinter solstice

The autumn equinox, around 22 September, marks the period when the hours of daylight and darkness are equal.

Thereafter, the nights are longer than the days and the year's energies begin to decline more rapidly.

Most animals respond by feverishly burying or hiding items, and finding a private 'cave' – sometimes under a table or in the airing cupboard – for their special retreat. They may also begin to eat noticeably more. This is a primal kickback to the wild, in case the local supermarket runs out of cat or budgie food during the long winter. Pets also instinctively carry food around at this time of the year while they are hoarding it. As they tend to scatter it, provide dried food, which will not make a mess.

Let them visit woodlands or, alternatively, bring some autumn foliage into the home. Gradually they will slow down and be less eager to go outdoors for long periods.

Winter

21 December–20 March (for the northern hemisphere), from the midwinter solstice to the spring equinox

The midwinter solstice – or the shortest day of the year, around 20–22 December – is the day when darkness reaches its peak, although thereafter the light slowly increases each day.

Animals may be reluctant to get out of bed and may become possessive about food they have left in their bowls. Once more, this is a throwback to the wild where it is important to conserve food so that there will be sufficient for the winter when food is scarce. Even normally active pets may be much slower than they usually are. They are not ill or unhappy, but just carrying out a mini-hibernation to conserve their strength for the spring, which is just around the corner. Give them extra bedding and take them for quiet walks or allow them access to the outdoors in whatever light remains.

In the next chapter we will look at healing and animals, both how our pets can help us through difficult times and how we can heal our pets' minor ills and problems through the loving bonds we share with them.

7 | Animals and healing

N O ONE FULLY UNDERSTANDS how healing takes place on a spiritual as well as a physical level, but the interconnection between mind, spirit and body seems to lie at the heart of healing illness and maintaining health. Traditional healing practices, which are still practised with a relatively unbroken tradition by some indigenous societies, understand that the well-being of the whole person is crucial to physical health, and conventional medical practice is also beginning to recognise this link. Recent research suggests that pet owners are healthier than non-pet owners, visiting doctors less frequently, having fewer colds and headaches, lower heart rates, blood pressure and cholesterol levels. In fact it is said that having a pet reduces your chances of having a heart attack, just as much as a low-salt diet or cutting down on alcohol.

One example of such findings comes from an item of research reported on 7 November 1999 by social psychologist Karen Allen to an American Heart Association meeting in Atlanta, Georgia. Researchers at the State University of New York at Buffalo, led by Dr Allen, studied 48 male and female stockbrokers who lived alone and were already taking Lycinprol, a medication for hypertension. Those in the study who either owned a pet or bought one during the research reduced by half the increase in blood pressure that came with stress.

Other research projects have shown that older people remain healthier if they own a pet, even if they do not have human company, while autistic children and stroke victims who are pet owners make greater progress than similarly affected people who do not spend time with animals.

PET HELPERS

Some dogs care for their sick and disabled owners on a regular basis. Although some are specially trained, ordinary dogs can also display quite amazing powers. Pixie is the pet dog of Adrian, who lives in Scotland. Adrian is confined to a wheelchair and suffers from an unusual and unpredictable form of diabetes that means he can fall into a coma without warning. Adrian obtained Pixie from a Scottish Society for the Protection of Animals rescue centre in 2001. In September 2002, Pixie was hailed as a heroine because she had saved Adrian's life five times in a year and prevented a number of hospitalisations by her prompt actions. Like the seizure dogs I mentioned on pages 35–6, Pixie is able to detect when Adrian's blood sugar level drops, though she has received no training. She becomes agitated, fussing over Adrian until he realises an attack is imminent and eats something to raise his blood sugar level. Adrian believed Pixie chose him because she showed him so much instant affection when he went to the rescue centre, in a way that the kennel helpers had not witnessed in her before.

On pages xiii–xvi, I described the almost magical rapport between Alan and his dog, Endal; they developed a high level of expertise through working together even though Endal was originally unable to be trained at the training centre. Endal and Alan were paired at the UK based charity Canine Partners for Independence, which trains dogs to assist disabled owners in a variety of ways, from loading and unloading a washing machine and paying at the supermarket checkout to working the buttons in a lift.

However, as with the story of Adrian and Pixie, it is the deep intuitive bond between owner and animal that is for me the most fascinating aspect of dogs that become united with a disabled owner to improve the quality of his or her life. Let me tell you the story of another remarkable pair, Hero, a golden retriever, and Gareth his owner, who live in Caldicot in Wales. They were also paired though Canine Partners for Independence and symbolise the very best of the human-animal bond.

Gareth is severely disabled after a car accident. However, his life was transformed by a dog from Canine Partners for Independence — an organisation that trains puppies to become assistance dogs. Each individual dog is partnered with a compatible owner, enabling the disabled person to live more independently and enjoy a far richer lifestyle. There are similar organisations throughout the world (see Resources). Gareth told me:

> Hero chose me; he took to me instantly. My girlfriend and I went to the Canine Partners for Independence training centre three or four times and met various dogs. But each time Hero came up to me and stayed at my side all during my visit. Others realised that he was 'my' dog before I did. What can I tell you about Hero? His tail wags with joy and he has a special smile — dog owners will know what I mean. He is totally in tune with what is required, as if he can anticipate my needs.
>
> Some of it is training. But when we went home, it was a new environment with different challenges and half the time it was Hero teaching *me*. I have a condition where I cannot feel anything below the chest, and if things go wrong I could get a life-threatening brain haemorrhage if the problem is not sorted — quickly. I have no symptoms, but somehow Hero senses when something is wrong and he stands and stares at me and will not stop till I get the message and take action. The dog tells me what I don't always know myself.
>
> Hero saved my life when my wheelchair got stuck in

the mud in a field. We had gone for a walk in the countryside near my home. It was 8.30 p.m., dark and cloudy and we were in a remote spot. Hero was enjoying playing in the field with his ball. But when I started to move off towards home, the wheels of the chair started spinning and I realised I was stuck. I went to call home on my mobile and realised the battery was flat. I had not told anyone where I was going. A side effect of my condition is that I cannot control my body temperature; I knew only Hero could save me, as I was rapidly getting cold and hypothermia would set in before I was found. I called Hero and attached his ball to the lead I had fastened to the wheelchair and he tugged it. He managed to pull hard enough to dislodge the chair from the mud.

We are never separated. If I can't take Hero somewhere, then I don't go. The first year I had Hero we had to go to the court hearing about the compensation for my injuries. It was very traumatic for me to relive the events of the accident in court but Hero was by my side, giving me the strength to put my case across. He sat beside me, understanding he had to be quiet but every so often he would look up at me and reassure me. Every time there was a recess and the judge went out, Hero would jump up and wag his tail. The hearing took three days and it was very lonely. I would not have coped without Hero.

Hero has instant understanding of what is needed in any situation. Although there are some basic commands, most of what he does is what I ask him to do and so he chooses to do it willingly and it gives him so much joy to help me. We have a corridor between the kitchen and my study. Before I had Hero, if I dropped something in the corridor I had to call for someone to help me. Having to be so dependent brought me a step down. Now, if Hero hears me drop something I hear his patter as he comes from another part of the house to retrieve it even before I have called him. He is so of full of joy to help that even something annoying like being unable to pick things up has become positive.

Sometimes, if I get cold, I am in constant pain. Usually, I try to take Hero out twice a day for a walk, and if I am having a good day he will prompt me when he wants to go out. But when the pain incapacitates me, I cannot take him out and he will never ask. He is almost closer to me when I am in pain. He climbs on to the bed and lies perfectly still next to me, his chin on my chest, and he will stay with me until I am better.

Hero is almost a part of me. He has made such a difference to my life. I have never experienced such emotion and care for others in a dog. When we are out somewhere and he is working he will not respond to other people. But if he sees someone who is disabled, especially a child, he lets me know that he wants to go over to him or her. Whenever I am down he reassures me, as though he is saying, not to worry we will sort it out, and we always do when Hero is by my side. Neither of us could do without the other now. Because of him I can face each day as it comes.

RECEIVING HEALING FROM ANIMALS

The stories I have told in this book about animals that help humans have all emphasised the pleasure animals derive from assisting their owners. You have probably noticed that if you are sick or unhappy your pets become much quieter than usual and cats or dogs may sit or lie quietly at your side, until the pain or sorrow passes. Whenever I have a bad gall bladder attack, my two female black cats sit like bookends at either end of the bed or sofa where I am lying.

If pain is bad or you feel the dark night of the soul descending, you can draw healing strength from your pets; dogs, cats, horses and rabbits are most receptive, but a bird that remains still for long periods can also give healing. If your animal doesn't respond automatically, remember to ask if he or she is able to help, as it may be feeling tired or out of sorts. But generally pets have great reserves of love that can be manifested as healing strength, and you will almost always sense their eagerness to help. Wait until the animal is very relaxed, perhaps in the early evening, and seek a quiet time and place where you can be alone or undisturbed. If discomfort or anxiety are keeping you awake, your cat or dog will not be far away and the silence of the night provides a good backdrop for receiving healing.

1 Sit or stand facing the animal and create a circuit by placing both your hands on either side of it.

2 Make eye contact, except with cats, which do not usually like to be stared at.

3 Keep perfectly still and focus on the animal's breathing for a minute or two until you are totally connected with the rhythm (see also page 70).

4 Deliberately push out of your mind everything except for the breathing, and, when you are ready, begin to breathe in time with the animal, even if it is slightly panting or purring.

5 On the in breath visualise a soft, pink light flowing from the animal into your body through the connection made with your power hand (the one you write with), and on the out breath allow visualise darkness flowing out of your receptive hand into the animal.

6 Keep up the pattern and you will find that in your mind's vision the darkness becomes lighter and the pink richer until eventually the flow of light is entirely pink.

7 Gradually picture the light fading, and slowly withdraw your hands from the animal.

8 You may both feel tired, so settle down together, or if you are working with a horse in a stable or a rabbit kept outdoors, make sure they are comfortable and have extra food.

9 Thank your pet.

If you have a sick animal, you can reverse the process by sending pink healing light through your hand into the pet's body and drawing out and transforming darkness with the other hand. Focus on the creature's breathing to establish the connection, as before, and you may notice it becomes easier as the healing light enters.

ANIMAL HEALERS

As with humans, the relationship between a creature's physical, emotional and spiritual well-being is very close and sometimes a physical problem may not be healing because of a spiritual trauma. Karen runs Merlin's Return, a wonderful New Age shop in Newport, Isle of Wight; she is an experienced animal and human healer, and described how she was called to visit a stallion that was not responding to treatment. She was able to communicate telepathically with him and discover the root cause of his continuing lameness. Karen told me:

> The horse was lame in both front legs and was not responding to conventional treatment. When I went to see him, the stallion communicated that he was lonely and distressed at seeing his filly mate, who had been in the next stable, have a heart attack and die. She had always been the leader when they were out to grass, and now that he no longer had a mate he did not want to canter round. I asked if he would like another mate and he said he could settle with another filly.
>
> The owner took in a rescued mare (it also was a leader and very bossy). The stallion's legs got better and the two trotted around together for many happy years afterwards.

Karen also left a snowflake obsidian crystal in the rafters of the stallion's stable to assist in his healing (see Appendix 1). Once the trauma of the stallion's witnessing his partner's death was recognised, self-healing, which had been blocked by grief, could begin on a physical level, just as with a human patient.

Any pet lover knows it is not fanciful to communicate as Karen did with a pet, although we may receive their feelings in our minds as images rather than words (see page 69 for how to talk to animals). Margaret, a former midwife who lives in Berkshire, is also a gifted human and animal healer. Her powers emerged quite spontaneously when her son Robbie became very ill with leukaemia. Sadly, although Margaret was able to help other very sick children, her own son died, though she was able to ease his pain and eventual passing. She said:

> I started a book in which I wrote the names of people who needed healing. I would visualise the people before me. Once I asked for healing for a cousin who was suffering with a bad back. I hadn't seen that branch of the family for a long time but my mother had mentioned my cousin was in constant pain. As I focused on my cousin, a very scruffy brown dog jumped out of nowhere into the room where I was working with my healing book.
>
> I gave healing to the dog as well and it vanished. The following week there was a family party and I went with my mother to see my aunt whose daughter had been suffering from a bad back. On the way, I asked my mother if my cousin had a dog.
>
> 'Yes, but it's been very ill and they were going to have it put down,' she replied. When we reached my aunt's house, a glossy brown dog bounded to the gate, wagging its tail. My cousin was walking without a trace of pain or stiffness.
>
> 'You must have used your magic on Penny as well,' my cousin laughed, pointing to the animal. 'She's been so much better since you sent me healing. In fact we took her to have her coat stripped this morning. She was really scruffy before, but we left her while she was so ill.'

After that, Margaret began to heal the animals belonging to friends and work colleagues who would bring their sick animals to work when she was on duty at the health centre. Indeed, one of the doctors complained that the surgery had become more like a vet's waiting room.

HEALING THROUGH THE LINK OF LOVE

Although there are many gifted animal healers and healing circles, you can heal your own pets, even if you have never worked with healing energies before, by using the strong channels of mutual love that already exist through which healing can be transmitted. If you talk very quietly to your pet, you may intuitively understand the problem, and, by sending love and light, you can alleviate the trauma and allow the animal's blocked self-healing mechanisms to spring back into action.

Much animal healing is spontaneous, and our desire to make a sick or distressed animal feel better or to ease its pain is transmitted automatically into their bodies as we stroke it gently or talk softly to soothe it. A number of spiritual healers of both animals and humans believe that we can draw down healing from a higher source to amplify our own innate healing abilities. You might ask for help from a favourite angel or archangel, from God or the Mother Goddess, a saint such as St Francis of Assisi, the Armenian St Blaise or the Irish St Bridget, all of whom are associated with animals and animal healing (St Francis and St Blaise are discussed further in Chapter 10).

The angels Hariel and Thiriel are said to protect pets and farm animals, whereas the angel Trgiaob protects and heals wild birds, and Jehiel protects wild animals. You can visualise these angels surrounded by animals and bathed in light, and if you close your eyes you will picture them in your own unique way. Alternatively, you may have a special deity or guardian spirit who cares for animals in your own faith. However, if this idea does not feel right for you, you can heal entirely through the positive love you experience between you and your pets and this is no less effective, for love from whatever source lies behind all forms of healing.

Healing a sick animal

If an animal has a broken limb or is unwell for more than two or three days, pet owners naturally seek veterinary advice. However, for chronic conditions or if a pet is simply off colour, sending healing energies is a natural response that needs no special training. You can also work to supplement conventional medicine or surgery. When you do need extra healing energy for your own animal, the following stages can be used. The method does not involve physical contact and so it can give extra strength when your pet is resting or is feeling crotchety and does not want to be touched. I have used this many times with my own animals.

1 Sit close to the animal or bird when he or she is asleep or totally relaxed.

2 Visualise a circle of light around the creature's body or, if you find this hard, use a fibre-optic lamp or a patch of natural sunlight or full moonlight and focus on a real pool of light surrounding your pet. Candles and animals tend not to be a good mix.

3 Silently repeat the animal's name several times, picturing the circle of light around the animal increasing in size and intensifying in brightness. If you wish, begin a simple mantra or chant either softly or in your mind, tapering slowly into silence. One I use calls on the powers of the natural world, which are very effective in healing animals: 'Light of love intensify, from the earth to the sky, healing power flow to me, from the rivers and the sea, bringing peace and harmony.' You can easily create your own healing blessings.

4 Within the circle of light, visualise your pet as strong and well again, and repeat his or her name silently three or four times.

5 You can now ask what healing you seek for the pet, and if you wish you can send it in the name of an angel, saint or deity or in the light of love. You may visualise or see in your mind the healing colours for animals – green, deep blue and pink – as rays of light surrounding your pet. Continue to picture this light breaking into beams and entering your pet in those places where there is pain or discomfort.

If the animal is in hospital for an operation or long-term treatment, you can carry out this healing prayer at the time of the treatment using a photograph or symbol and visualise the healing colours passing into that. You can also use a picture of a wild animal or bird to send healing to an individual or to an endangered species. If, however, your pet dies, it does not mean that your healing has failed; healing can bring a gentle passing, if recovery would have left your beloved pet with a poor quality of life.

UNDERSTANDING A PET'S ILLNESS

Earlier in this chapter, I described how Karen understood intuitively the stallion's distress that was blocking the self-healing process for his lameness. Sometimes the external signs of an illness are clear; for example, a limp that does not respond to treatment. But at others we may instinctively feel a pet is unwell even if there are no outward symptoms. If we can learn to trust our instinctive wisdom then we can often catch a problem before it becomes more serious. For example, Rosemary, who lives on the Isle of Wight, described to me how her daughter, Sue, recounted a dream in which their dog, Barney, had a bad tooth that made him so ill he died. Rosemary reassured her daughter that the dog was fine as he was eating normally and was not obviously in pain. But on her daughter's insistence Rosemary looked into Barney's mouth and there was a tooth that was slightly blackened. She took Barney to the vet who found an abscess beneath the tooth that was so bad that if it had been left untreated it would have led to septicaemia.

If you feel worried about an animal, and the feeling is different from a free-floating anxiety, trust your instincts and visit the vet, or at least keep a close eye on the animal. Owners are very tuned in to their pets, just as mothers are to their children. Dreams are just one way our unconscious minds can alert us to possible trouble.

In the next chapter we will look at ways of using crystals, herbs and flower essences to help with healing your pets.

8 | Crystals, flower essences and herbs for healing

W E CAN USE THE special healing properties of crystals, flower essences and herbs to help our pets when they are unwell. In the same way as humans, animals can benefit from the gentle energies that crystals and flower essences contain. They can be safely given to animals and birds as necessary. Herbal remedies are stronger, however, and we need to practise care when we administer them to pets.

CRYSTALS AND ANIMALS

Crystals are a very safe method of animal healing, especially for the beginner, since absolutely nothing is taken internally and you do not have to worry about dosages or prohibitions. We do not fully understand why crystals should be as effective as they are for healing animals and birds as well as people. One explanation may be that because crystals are formed over millions of years in the earth by the action of volcanic fire, water and wind, they seem to transfer vitality that animals can easily absorb. In practice, even in the hands of someone who has never healed or used crystals before, they seem to amplify both the healing energies of the healer and the self-healing powers of the patient.

Crystals are also helpful in maintaining the health and well-being of your pets and of transmitting healing light to animals or birds even if they are not present when the healing work takes place.

USING CRYSTALS FOR HEALTH AND WELL-BEING

If you have not used crystals before, leave small dishes of mixed green, brown, golden and orange crystals around the home for two or three weeks near to where the pet usually sits or sleeps, or if you have a horse place them in the stable. You can place a single stone of any of these colours in a birdcage or small animal cage or a fish or reptile tank. Small tumbled or polished crystals are easily obtainable from gift as well as mineral stores and are ideal for this purpose.

After only a few days you will probably notice your pets are not only calmer but also have more focused energy and enthusiasm for life. If the crystals are in a central place in your home, the improvement may extend throughout the human family.

On pages 67–9, I described crystals that give life and restore colour to the aura. Of course, that is just one way of explaining how crystalline energies benefit animals. Some owners regularly give their pets water to drink, in which a soft green jade crystal has been soaked, to maintain health – a belief that goes back thousands of years to ancient China and is still current today. Jade is traditionally believed to bring long life and health to animals and humans. It also seems to calm a hyperactive pet when regularly drunk as jade water.

Turquoise is another crystal traditionally used in animal welfare. It can be fixed to pets' collars, to the bridles of horses and to the mirrors of caged birds to prevent the animals getting lost or straying, or being stolen. It also seems to act as a charm against accidents, the malice of animal haters and the ill effects of harmful pollutants (see Appendix 1).

If you take in an animal from a rescue centre that has

been neglected or ill-treated, you can help persuade it to stay by placing unpolished chunks of rose quartz and jade near to the entrances to your home; also set rose quartz in an empty food bowl between feeds, after it has been washed, and under the corners of a pet sleeping area, to replace bad memories and gradually restore trust (see pages 151–8 and Appendix 1 for a full list of crystal healing properties).

HEALING YOUR PETS WITH PAIRS OF CRYSTALS

You can also use a pair of crystals of similar shape and size with complementary qualities as an effective way to transmit health-restoring energies to a pet, even if you are a relatively inexperienced healer. The crystals are held in each hand, but it does not matter which crystal you have in which hand, as the energies will flow between them.

Choosing your crystal pairs

Keep two special crystals especially for healing your pet, or you might like to use different pairs according to whatever feels right at the time. You can visit a mineral, New Age or gift shop and hold different crystals until you sense what works for you. The stones should be round and quite flat and of equal size. The size will depend on the size of animal. For horses there are some wonderful palm stones – flat crystals that fit inside the palm of your hand. Polished or tumbled stones can be used for any creature.

The following are very effective for any creature in the animal or bird kingdom including reptiles and even stick insects. I have listed the special strengths of the suggested pairs, but you may find that one pair works well on your pet no matter what the problem:

Green jade and orange amber: for restoring energy after a chronic or long-lasting illness and for health maintenance in older animals or birds.

Purple amethyst or jade and rose quartz: for creatures that have suffered abuse or neglect in the past or that have been involved in an accident or a bad fight or bullying.

Pink manganocalcite, or a very pale ordinary pink calcite and a pale blue lace agate: for pets that are very timid and fearful, whether of people, other animals, noises or places, for throat and chest problems and for healing small or very young animals and birds.

Brown or grey smoky quartz and apache tear (transparent black obsidian) through which you can see the light: for very old or very sick creatures. These can ease their last days until they are emotionally ready to let go of life.

White or creamy moonstone, cloudy white selenite and a soft-blue angelite: for pregnant or new mothers and the newborn, for all hormonal and fertility problems, especially in female creatures and for calming down hyperactivity.

Green moss agate or green and white tree agate with black and white snowflake obsidian: for problems with bones, muscles and joints, for pain relief and problems with growth, such as fur.

Banded brown agate and yellowy-gold rutilated quartz: for skin problems, allergies and digestive disorders, also for curbing aggressive or destructive behaviour.

Alternatively use a pair of creamy or matching yellow or pink quartz you find on the seashore, on a riverbank or a hillside. These are filled with earth, water and sky power and so are good for any animal or bird healing. The following, paired with a brown or pink banded agate, rose quartz or jade have become associated with particular species:

Cat's eye, either yellow or green: for healing cats.

Aquamarine or blue, red or pink coral: for circling over a fish tank or pond

Dalmatian jasper, black and fawn spotted jasper: for dogs

Falcon's eye, a blue or green tiger's eye: for birds

Leopardskin jasper, mottled brown, grey or black: for exotic pets, such as snakes and lizards, and insects

WORKING WITH YOUR CRYSTAL PAIRS

Before you begin healing, practise slowly revolving the crystal you are holding in your power hand – the one you write with – clockwise and the one in the other hand anticlockwise at the same time to set up a rhythm.

Beginning healing

Sunset is a good time for removing pain and illness and for inducing calm, while the early morning helps the crystal to infuse an exhausted, unhappy or sick animal with energy or optimism. But in practice you can heal at any time, though natural sunlight makes crystal healing easier. If the day is dark, a fibre-optic lamp will increase light power. You can also try full moonlight.

1 Sit quietly with the animal, stroking and talking quietly until he or she settles. Or you can wait until the animal is settled or sleeping.

2 Kneel or sit near the animal, or for a horse stand about 12–15 centimetres (4½–6 inches) away; many creatures find the power of even a gentle crystal too strong for direct contact.

3 Revolve your crystal pairs, clockwise and anticlockwise together, allowing your hands to guide you.

4 Work from the tail upwards, and hold the crystal a few centimetres away from the body as you work – creatures seem to prefer this.

5 You may feel yourself entering a light, relaxed state in which movement becomes totally spontaneous and entirely smooth.

6 Murmur soothingly as you work and visualise dull, grey light leaving the animal and misty white light entering. Allow words to come and you may begin a soft chant quite spontaneously.

7 If there is any area where there is discomfort or problems, you can work lightly two or three centimetres (¾–1¼ inches) above the painful spot.

8 If an animal is naturally oversensitive or becomes easily excited, you can sit facing the animal and work on a visualised outline of the creature in front of you.

9 Gradually you will sense the crystal energy weakening, and at this point you should slow down gradually and stop.

10 Sit quietly with the animal for a few minutes and you may be rewarded by a glow around him or her, even if you do not normally try to see auras clearly.

11 Repeat the healing when necessary.

After healing wash the crystal pairs under running water, leaving them to dry naturally, if possible in sun- or moon-light. When not in use keep them near the place the animal sleeps or rests so that the crystals can absorb the creature's unique essence.

FLOWER ESSENCES

Another form of healing where you are not using medication, flower essences will in no way interfere with conventional, professional herbal or homeopathic treatment. Unlike herbal medicine, the flower essence is made from the essences of blossoms or leaves, floated on pure water in sun- or moonlight to absorb, it is believed, the energy pattern of the flower or tree used. Thus the finished essence does not contain any medicinal properties on a physical level. Rather it seems to affect the emotional and spiritual state of the creature positively, so perhaps triggering self-healing.

Marlene Keel is director of the International Flower Essence Centre in Victoria, Australia, a company that specialises in flower essences for animals and birds. I asked her why she considers flower essences to be so useful for animals. She replied:

> Our pets, by and large, react to our own emotional states. For example, observe your dog on a day when you might be feeling a little miserable. First, he'll probably try to cheer you up by bestowing multitudinous licks on your face. If this fails, he is likely to curl up sadly at your feet, mirroring your mood. Essences are great to relieve the negative feelings your pet/animal is experiencing. They subtly resolve issues, promote a more positive frame of mind and offer relief and comfort to the animal.
>
> Like us, animals respond to other things in their environment and life; for example, aggressive animals, excess noise, solitude, etc. Again, you can administer essences to help them resolve and release the negative emotions such events or environments can cause.
>
> Essences are also of value to assist the animals in resolving conflicts that exist when several pets live under the one roof. Try always to be aware of where your pet is at emotionally and spiritually. It is good to learn and recognise problems that exist in their lives. By recognising patterns, you can help prepare your pet for those times when a bit of emotional support would be beneficial. You could then organise the right essence(s) for their specific needs in advance.

Marlene Keel has special essences for different stress and problem states that are suitable for pets, large and small, fur and feathered. However, other practitioners use ordinary flower essences, for example, the Bach remedies, for healing animals.

If you have not used flower remedies before, try an all-purpose remedy; for example, Dr Bach's Five Flower Rescue Remedy, made from cherry plum, clematis, impatiens, star of Bethlehem and rock rose. It will ease almost any sudden trauma from a visit to the vet (administer before and after), any bad experiences, such as an attack by another animal, or emotional upset when moving house.

Dr Bach's Rescue Remedy can be used for any creature; there is even a Rescue Cream that is helpful when rubbed on horses' sprains, and is especially good for highly strung horses, as it seems to calm them instantly. I successfully treated a friend's bald guinea pig with Dr Bach's Rescue Remedy and in a few weeks not only did the fur grow back but also the highly excitable animal was calm and much more amenable to being handled.

FLOWER ESSENCES IN PRACTICE

We do not really understand how flower remedies or essences work, but thousands of pet owners as well as professional animal healers use them regularly because they are found to be safe but effective. You may find them especially helpful at times when an animal develops a psychosomatic illness, or has a skin condition caused or made worse by stress, or if it is unable to sleep or rest or seems fearful without reason.

On pages 165–9 I have suggested some flower essences that I and other animal healers consider to be helpful. There is a whole range of material about flower essences on the Internet and a number of vets are recognising that alternative treatments do seem beneficial. Any that are used for humans are fine for pets, though you may want to dilute them in water, especially when using them with small animals. You can add a drop or two of the chosen remedy to a bowl of pet water, into food, on to a grooming brush or in a pet bath. If the animal is very small or delicate, add just three or four drops to 250 millilitres (8 fluid ounces) of water and place it in a silent spray – the kind that does not upset animals – and spray pet bedding or the room where the pet sleeps.

You can use flower and tree remedies on birds in the wild as well as on pets, by adding a single drop to the drinking water you leave for them. You can also sprinkle a flower remedy dissolved in water around a pet stable or bed to keep him or her safe while sleeping. You can't give too big a dose, and in fact informal experiments have discovered that even a tiny amount of essence has the same effect as a larger quantity.

HERBAL MEDICINE AND PETS

I have left herbal remedies until last because they do need more care, but they are, nevertheless, a valuable tool for pet healthcare. In the wild, animals naturally eat herbs that are good for specific disorders. Bears and monkeys are especially gifted, and at the Monkey World at Wareham in Dorset, a sanctuary for rescued primates, medicinal herbs are grown in or near the enclosures; on more than one occasion a monkey has anticipated a remedy by plucking a herb, later prescribed by a vet for its illness.

Of course, you cannot just use human herbal remedies on pets without taking care. For example, white willow is used in aspirin for humans as a general pain relief and also to relieve arthritic pain; however, it is toxic for some animals, especially cats. A seemingly harmless herbal medication that needs care is garlic; used in excess, garlic can lead to anaemia in animals, but in moderation it is good for animal hearts and fat levels and to boost the immune system as well as repelling and killing parasites. However, many of the herbs humans accept today as part of our green pharmacy are beneficial for animals and birds.

PET HERBAL REMEDIES IN EVERYDAY LIFE

Go into any large pet shop and you will see tea tree tooth-paste for dogs, parsley and peppermint chews to sweeten breath and aid digestion, herbal flea collars containing pennyroyal, eucalyptus and lavender, pet dinners with sage and thyme to strengthen an animal against infection, catnip balls containing leaves and blossoms to give cats energy and a sense of well-being, tea tree lotion for use against ring-worm and other fungal infections and peppermint tinctures to prevent travel sickness. All these are ancient herbs used by our ancestors in animal husbandry, and if your pets can have access to a selection of beneficial herbs they will instinctively eat those that their body needs at particular times and will not eat any that are harmful. The following herbs are a useful selection, and can even be grown in pots: mint, chamomile, echinacea, rosemary, sage, thyme and milk thistle. Herbs growing wild near a road may be polluted by fumes and so are less suitable.

Herbal remedies may be more suitable for animals because they find them gentler on their systems than pharma-ceutical remedies; for example, flea collars containing powerful pesticides can give pets skin irritation and also make human family members wheeze.

ADMINISTERING HERBAL REMEDIES

A number of vets are happy to prescribe herbal remedies. If not there are many reliable homeopathic and alternative pet practitioners who can give you advice if you wish to try these older remedies; many been used for hundreds of years, and in some cases thousands of years.

The problem with home diagnosis of a pet when using herbal remedies is that the animal does not recognise the composition of a pill or tincture and so the instinctive protec-tive mechanism against eating what is toxic or may cause an allergic reaction is greatly diminished. Therefore, we owners have to monitor products on their behalf. Read labels on any herbal remedies, and even vitamin and mineral supplements. If in doubt ask a herbalist or a reputable pet shop if the rem-edies are suitable for a particular species of animal or bird, what dosage should be used and how often. Some herbs are not suitable for pregnant or nursing animals, so always check.

Use several doses at regular intervals rather than a single large one. As with humans, do not administer any particular herb continuously over long periods, otherwise immunity will build up; two weeks on and one week off is a useful rule of thumb. Do not use externally applied remedies near to the eyes or genitals.

In the next chapter we will consider what happens when an animal dies, and we will look at ways of easing the grief and perhaps in time learning to love another pet.

9 | When a pet dies

WHILE RESEARCHING THIS BOOK I was told of an anonymous passage of prose that described how pets that die wait for their owners near Rainbow Bridge so that they can cross together into heaven. The passage has inspired a number of Internet sites, poems and books and it has been helpful to a number of owners who have lost beloved pets, especially those that died unexpectedly. I will quote part of it and only regret I cannot credit the source. Although some might say it is sentimental, the concept of the Rainbow Bridge is one way of expressing the enduring love between pets and humans.

Just this side of heaven is a place called Rainbow Bridge.

When an animal dies that has been especially close to someone here, that pet goes to Rainbow Bridge. There are meadows and hills for all of our special friends so they can run and play together. There is plenty of food, water and sunshine, and our friends are warm and comfortable.

All the animals who had been ill and old are restored to health and vigour; those who were hurt or maimed are made whole and strong again, just as we remember them in our dreams of days and times gone by.

The animals are happy and content, except for one

small thing; they each miss someone very special to them, who had to be left behind.

They all run and play together, but the day comes when one suddenly stops and looks into the distance. His bright eyes are intent; his eager body quivers. Suddenly he begins to run from the group, flying over the green grass, his legs carrying him faster and faster.

You have been spotted, and when you and your special friend finally meet, you cling together in joyous reunion, never to be parted again. The happy kisses rain upon your face; your hands again caress the beloved head, and you look once more into the trusting eyes of your pet, so long gone from your life but never absent from your heart.

Then you cross Rainbow Bridge together ...

LOSING A PET IN DEATH

Most of us have experienced the death of a beloved pet, and whether it resulted from an accident, a sudden illness or was a gradual passing, the grief can remain acute for months and even years afterwards. If a pet is very sick or old, you may decide it is kindest to discontinue veterinary treatment except to make sure the animal is pain free and comfortable. It is one of the hardest things in the world to take an animal to be put to sleep, but sometimes they can indicate their readiness to move on by ceasing to eat or just by lying motionless and unresponsive. Unlike humans, animals have no fear of death, except if they are in situations where they witness the slaughter of other creatures.

My very old white cat, Haegl, which I had as a kitten, became chronically unwell when she was 13 years old, and so diminished was her quality of life that I realised I was keeping her alive for my sake. When I got out the pet carrier to take Haegl to the vet, she climbed inside and lay down quietly, although she had always hated being confined. She did not react to any other animals in the waiting room, which was also unusual, and on the table in the surgery she lay down and rolled over on her side, looking at me with much peace and love as the injection was given.

Even if we are not with an animal when it dies, our strong bond can enable us to share, and perhaps spiritually ease, their passing with our love. Cindy, who lives in Sussex, told me how she lost her dog Honey:

> On 17 September 1991, my husband decided he would take our two dogs out for a walk. I could not go because my seven-month-old twins were asleep and I did not want to wake them. While I was doing my housework I was thinking about one of my dogs, Honey. I was washing up at the sink when suddenly I felt as if someone had punched me in the chest. It was as if a dark cloud had suddenly descended, and at the same time my back was shuddering and went cold. I knew something dreadful had happened. I looked at the clock and the time was 11.04.
>
> My husband arrived home about half an hour later, and as he walked into the kitchen, he was trying to fight back the tears. He said, 'Honey's dead.' I ran to the window and could see Honey lying in the back of the car.
>
> I did not stop crying for weeks. I later discovered that the dogs were chasing each other as usual. Honey hid in the long grass, but as she jumped she went straight over the cliff edge, about 70 feet down on to a shingle and stone beach. The accident must have happened at about 11.04 because just a minute or two beforehand my husband had checked his watch and it was just past 11.00 a.m.

EASING THE PASSING

Gradually we may become aware that an animal or bird is slowly letting life go. Unlike creatures in the wild, a pet may not know how to find a peaceful place to spend their last hours, and so you may need to create a sanctuary with old bedding that can be disposed of afterwards with sheets of newspaper underneath in case the animal cannot make it out-doors or to a litter tray. If possible, this sanctuary should be a quiet room, a garage or a comfortable outbuilding where there will be little noise or disturbance.

Witnessing a pet peacefully easing into death can be a good way for adults and children to lose any fear of dying. Some animals may choose a corner in the house. Other animals in the family may groom the dying animal, even if they have previously seemed indifferent or hostile towards it; if not they may just leave the animal in peace.

Provide water and a little food, which you can replace regularly, even if it is not touched, and ring the area with dark brown stones or crystals, such as dark agates, obsidian or jet, smoky quartz or apache tear to envelop the animal in peace. Check on your pet regularly and stay with him or her when you sense he or she wants company or for you to sleep close by. A night or two in a sleeping bag is a small price to pay for sharing these last precious moments. Allow the family to visit the pet quietly; even small children can be amazingly sensi-tive and still when they visit a very sick animal.

Place a favourite blanket and toys nearby and one of your own garments so your pet does not feel abandoned when you cannot be there. Talk softly to it, saying that you know he or she wants to leave and that they must go when they are ready. Sometimes we can unwittingly hold an animal back from dying by our desire not to let it go; pets are very loyal and can sense this in us, and so even though it is very ill your pet may try to prolong its life for your sake. You may find the animal becomes gradually quieter and still. When the end comes, leave the animal for a while and then wrap him or her in a favourite blan-ket with a toy and allow the family to say their goodbyes.

PET FUNERALS

Bury the animal within a short time of death or, if you have no land, ask a vet you know if they would kindly take the animal away. You could then create a small memorial place with flowers and a photograph in the pet's favourite place within the home. In many parts of the world there are also pet cemeteries, usually situated in natural woodland or a field, where your pet's body can be returned to the earth.

Children especially benefit from witnessing the burial of a pet and organising a service, whether in a pet cemetery, in the garden or a favourite piece of woodland (bury the pet deep enough so that wild animals will not disturb it). In this way children can see the animal's body being returned to the earth. If you plant living flowers or a small bush on top of the grave, they can readily understand the process of new life.

Even young children can organise a funeral service; this can be directed to whomever you consign the spirit of your pet: God, the Goddess, St Francis, an angel or the positive forces of light. Adults too benefit from a special service of remembrance, where they can recall aloud all the happy, funny times they enjoyed with the animal.

If children are grieving deeply you might like to light a candle at the same time each night during the following few evenings. Place it next to a picture or memento of the animal, and make sure the candle is in a safe place. The children can share a favourite memory and then blow out the candle, sending it to the animal wherever he or she is. (Remember never to leave a burning candle unattended and to be especially careful when young children are around.) Before long the children will be too busy or will forget to light the candle with you, and the next stage of their healing process can begin quite naturally.

Do not, however, be afraid to grieve yourself for as long as you would for any loved friend. Those who say, 'It was only an animal. Pull yourself together' have never lost a loved pet. You may wish to remember by going to the animals' favourite place outdoors and placing a few flowers there. Alternatively, light a white candle near to the pet photograph and spend a little time recalling fond memories.

ARE ANIMALS FOR EVER?

Most of us can recall the softness of a departed pet's fur and its distinctive sounds and smells. But some people are convinced that they see or sense a pet after death, sometimes at a time when they are alone or frightened. I was intrigued by the story sent to me in October 2002 by Anne, who lives in Exeter. She explained:

> I am very nervous about walking through the local underpass, especially at night. But one evening a month ago I had no choice, because I was completely exhausted and couldn't face the long walk to avoid it. As I started through the tunnel, a black and white mongrel dog frisked up to me and started to walk with me as if providing an escort. I spoke to him, saying how much he looked like my old dog, Flash, who died last year.
>
> As I reached the steps of the exit, the dog stopped, looked up at me and wagged his tail. I patted him and had a terrible shock when my hand encountered thin air. The dog had vanished! I am not saying it definitely was Flash, but I think it was. He was definitely not of this world.

Such tales might seem strange to anyone who is not a pet owner or animal lover. But animals are such amazingly wonderful creatures that I sometimes feel we have more to learn from them than they from us. If there were a purpose in a pet's return it would surely be to help us, just as it had in life.

ANIMALS AND SURVIVAL AFTER DEATH

There are great philosophical debates as to whether an animal has a soul. However, I believe they have, because I have received so many accounts over the past 15 years of animals that have been seen or sensed after their death. Furthermore, the courageous and altruistic deeds animals carry out to protect and save the lives of humans and other animals suggest that they do indeed have noble feelings and not simply instincts. This must surely mean that they too merit a place in heaven.

The church's view on animal souls can be ambivalent. However, in July 1998 the Irish bishop Pat Buckley commented: 'There will indeed be animals in heaven. I recently heard an expert on the supernatural talk about the intuition and extra-sensory perception that animals possess. She told one story of an old man, who was dying in hospital:

> Suddenly he sat up in his hospital bed and called out: 'Sandy – let's go for a walk' and then lay down and died. His faithful dog was being minded by a family ten miles away. It lay down on the floor and died at exactly the same time as the old man. Obviously the old man's spirit and the dog's spirit were one.

What impressed the bishop most, however, was the case of Scarlett, the New York cat that saved her five kittens from a blazing building. She returned five times into the flames, even though her eyes were swollen with blisters and her fur and paws were burned, and carried each one out in her mouth. The bishop commented: 'Many of we human beings might not be able to show such love. I cannot imagine the God of love allowing an animal like Scarlett to simply disappear at the end of her life, to vanish into dust and ashes. Why would such innocent and loving animals not get to heaven whereas weak humans can get there?' I agree with Bishop Buckley as I, too, have heard similar stories.

Animal ghosts

I have found many accounts of people who momentarily see, sense or feel a beloved pet in their home, particularly on the anniversary of its death; other animals present may stare intently at a corner of the room and wag their tails or purr. Janette, who lives in Hawkes Bay, New Zealand, described how this happened to her family on a number of occasions. Evelyn Gregory, a UK author and broadcaster, who has researched this field extensively, has allowed me to reproduce Janette's account:

> Nine years ago I was given a black and white kitten which I called Mushki. Her one foible was that she considered herself to be human which extended to creeping in under the bedclothes at night so that when I woke I would find her tucked up with her head on the pillow snoring. We lived on the outskirts of a coastal city in New Zealand in a semi-rural area. In March 1990, Mushki was killed while crossing the road one night. Shortly afterwards my mother saw her run up our lawn and disappear. One morning my father was woken by the sound of a cat meowing and turned to see Mushki standing at the door. No other cats were indoors at the time. Even the dog would often look at nothing and begin barking and wagging her tail.
>
> ... one night I woke suddenly as something jumped on my bed, walked along beside me, lay down and began purring. It took several minutes to convince myself it was only that I had felt the duvet slipping off. When I felt down and put on the light, the duvet was in place and an invisible but physical presence was curled up beside me. It was Mushki.
>
> Even now she will turn up when least expected. One explanation is that since she died so suddenly and unexpectedly, she is trying to reassure me that she is fine. When she was alive she would always jump up for a cuddle if any of the family were upset.

Sometimes people may see the ghost of an unfamiliar animal. Children are especially receptive to this because they are psychically more open than adults. When Angie, who lives on the Isle of Wight, was young she stayed overnight in a house in Berkshire. During the night a big black dog insisted on jumping on the bed, in spite of being pushed off several times. In the morning Angie asked where the dog was. The owners of the house said that they used to have a black dog but it had died some years before.

MAKING CONTACT WITH ANIMAL GHOSTS

Some people would not wish to see an animal after its death but prefer to cherish their memories and photographs. If it would upset you to see or sense your animal, then you will not have such an experience. A pet would not wish to distress you after its death any more than it would have in life. A possible explanation why people see the ghost of their pet is that its love and essential personality is somehow etched on the home and this can be activated occasionally if an owner is thinking about the pet.

You can induce these experiences, whether you consider that the soul of a pet can return or if you are visualising its presence as part of your healing process. The following suggestions will help you:

- Call the pet's name softly when you are in a favourite spot in the garden, a sunny corner where your cat slept or on a familiar walk. Recall in your mind's eye the colour of its eyes and the colour and texture of the fur, ears and tail. Remember also its bark or meow.

- Focus in your mind's vision on a small patch of animal fur and gradually widen your mental image until you can visualise the whole animal. Walk on or move away and then turn round quickly and you may momentarily feel his or her fur or catch a quick glimpse of your pet.

- Recall actual smells associated with the pet; for example, damp fur drying by a radiator after rain. You may even be able to visit places where the smells evoke a strong memory; for example, a patch of lavender or newly mown grass where the animal used to roll.

- Use textures as triggers: trampling through a pile of autumn leaves, rubbing a rough towel you dried the animal with against your skin or stroking another animal's fur in warm sunlight.

- In the early morning or evening, find a patch of sunlight or create a circle of light with a large, golden candle. Place your hands within the circle of light and stroke your animal at the height he or she was in life, moving your hands slowly and rhythmically, and murmuring the words of endearment that you used with your pet when you were alone. Stare at the brightness and then close your eyes and open them rapidly to *see* your pet momentarily in the after-image. (Remember, never leave a burning candle unattended.)

- Before sleep, hold a photograph showing the animal in a favourite place, and imprint every image on to your memory so that when you close your eyes you can see the photograph clearly in your mind's vision. Just before sleep visualise the place and the pet clearly and superimpose yourself in the picture. Walk in your mind together into sleep and you may dream of the animal.

- Go to places where you hear noises associated with the pet: rooks cawing on a favourite walk across fields, the clatter of horse's hooves, a cockerel crowing, other dogs barking. This time, using your inner ear, superimpose the unique sound of your pet. In that moment you may feel close, and for a second you may hear your animal's snuffle in your mind.

ANIMALS AS GUARDIANS

On page 118 I described how Anne's dog, Flash, apparently came back to protect her. However, for Lilian a former family dog became a guardian spirit of the family over generations. Lilian wrote to me:

A legend runs in my family of a spirit dog, a black one. My father came from Hull in Yorkshire. His mother said to my mother when she was still courting: 'When you get married and have children, if you see the black dog things will go very well.'

Mum and Dad married years later and thought no more about it until Mum was in labour with my eldest sister in 1949. It was a home birth. My mum asked my dad to fetch the midwife. As he raced along the street, Dad heard a panting behind him. He felt terrified and the hairs on the back of his neck and arms stood up. He knocked on the midwife's door and her husband answered. A black dog rushed past them, up the stairs and into the midwife's room, jumped on the bed, panted and disappeared, as if it knew it had found the right person. Later the midwife related the tale to my mother. She said she had never experienced anything like it before in all her years of nursing.

Two years later my mother was expecting me. Again it was a home birth and the midwife saw the black dog again. This time she lifted it off the bonnet of her car and then it disappeared.

Such stories are by their nature mysterious. But they may indicate that the love and care of pets does sometimes seem to last for ever.

ANIMALS THAT GRIEVE FOR THEIR OWNERS

This link of love exists both ways in the pet/human relationship. If a pet remains alive after the death of its beloved owner, he or she may maintain the tie of loyalty across the dimensions. Many people have heard the tale of Greyfriars Bobby, a Skye terrier who, after his master John Grey's death in Edinburgh, sat at the graveside in Greyfriars churchyard in all weathers for 14 years. Locals built the dog a shelter in the church grounds and made sure he was fed. After Bobby died, Baroness Burdett Coutts had a statue of the loyal dog erected in the churchyard.

It was not until I read of Rupert Sheldrake's research that I realised just how remarkable this true story was. Rupert Sheldrake pointed out that the only way the dog could have identified the grave was through telepathic bonds. How could a dog like Bobby not be reunited with his master after his own death?

There is another wonderful story about how an animal shared the dying moments of his beloved owner. Sitting Bull, the wise man of the Lakota Sioux Tribe, was killed in a battle against the US federal government. As Sitting Bull fell from his horse and lay dying on the battlefield, his white horse did not run away. It had once performed in the circus, and on the battlefield it began dancing on its hind legs and circling its master as though performing in the ring, while the bullets rained. The horse continued to dance round its dead master even after the battle was over, until it fell exhausted.

HELPING ANIMALS TO GRIEVE

Whether a human family member or another household animal dies, we can sometimes forget how deeply a surviving animal may be suffering because of the loss.

It can be good for children in the household to spend extra time with a grieving pet, as this can give mutual comfort at a time of loss. Sometimes when people are rushing round after a family death, children can feel redundant, so this can be helpful to them. They can also work though their unhappiness at the death of another family pet by cheering up the surviving one.

The bereaved creature may benefit from being allowed to sleep with a garment or blanket belonging to the deceased person or animal. However, he or she may not want to sleep alone and will indicate if it would like to sleep by your bed for a while. In time, confidence and independence will return – temporarily indulging a bereaved pet is very different from spoiling a young animal.

If its former owner was elderly and the pet has to be taken from its own home to that of the deceased person's relations, it is important to take as many familiar items with it as possible, such as feeding bowls and bedding. The animal will need a quiet place with its own things in its new home. As it will be very bewildered, it will initially need to be away from other pets. If you know the creature's routine, try to keep to it, and if you live near to its former home try to keep to familiar walks for a while. Given kindness, patience and care the animal may settle in time. If its owner was someone we loved and lost, the pet may gradually provide a continuing link with that person for us. However, some very old animals may not survive the loss of an owner with whom they have lived for years.

If you take an animal from a rescue centre and its previous owner died, the centre may well have the animal's own feeding utensils and perhaps some mementoes that they could give you to ease the transition. Your kindness and care will help it to settle.

In the next chapter we will look at how we can discover and get to know the wildlife that lives in our gardens and local parks.

10 | Wildlife in the park and garden

WILDLIFE HAS ALWAYS LIVED in cities. However, since the 1990s the numbers of urban wild animals, birds and fish have increased greatly, thanks to programmes by local government and conservation organisations to purify once-polluted rivers and canals, to plant trees and bushes and to protect marshlands to offer shelter to small animals and birds. For example, during the 1980s the habitats of wild otters in the UK were endangered even in remote countryside, owing to industrial pollution and destruction by land developers of natural plant life along the sides of rivers, and the otters were threatened with extinction. However, since the late 1990s otters have returned to rivers and canals in the UK. Furthermore, they have been seen right in the centre of towns from where they had disappeared years ago; for example, along canal and river banks in the centre of Leeds, Bristol, Norwich, Doncaster, Newcastle and Glasgow.

Other creatures have adapted to urban living, such as a fox family living behind the buffers of Platform 1 at Paddington Station in the centre of London, and in abandoned cars in Glasgow. Peregrine falcons now nest in the ruins of the once famous Battersea Power Station, no more than a mile or two from the Houses of Parliament in central London. I have written mainly about places I know well, but similar programmes are in force in urban areas all over the world.

ENCOUNTERING INDIGENOUS WILDLIFE

The relationship between humans and animals and birds living wild is complex, but can be very fruitful for both sides. Encountering local wildlife is a privilege and very uncertain. Wild creatures will approach when we are still and silent and, if they come into gardens, may accept food or shelter. But it is because they are wild that we must meet them on their terms, however friendly they may seem; they must for their own survival remain undomesticated. It is truly a blessing from nature to share a few moments of quiet companionship as a wild creature's world touches ours before the creature disappears into the darkness or scampers up a tree. We need to be very patient if we are to be rewarded with even a momentary connection, and must adapt to their timescale to make this happen; we need to be there in the early morning, at sunset and after dark, as many small animals are nocturnal. Of course there are exceptions, and small creatures, such as hedgehogs, may become almost one of the family if regularly fed.

For years my human family had a pair of hedgehogs in our garden, Holly and Prickles. At some point they had rolled in blue paint, which remained, harmlessly, on their spikes, distinguishing them from visiting hedgehogs. Their mission in life was to become house-hogs and they would lurk in the bushes or hide behind large plant pots waiting for the back door to open, so they could enter the living room. When apprehended, the intrepid pair would break ranks, one scuttling behind the sofa, the other seeking refuge behind the cooker in the kitchen; they would squeal indignantly when evicted.

On one occasion I came into the living room to the sound of shrieks. While watching television my 14-year-old son, Jack, had put his bare foot on Holly – the hedgehog was sprawled on the mat in front of the television, presumably approving of Jack's choice of channel. On another occasion, Jack was asleep in his bedroom downstairs one night when he awoke to see his boxer shorts walking across the room. Curious, he sat up, only to witness his T-shirt, which he had abandoned on the floor, following likewise, being dragged by Prickles in the process of setting up camp in the corner for the night. Eventually the house-hogs stopped coming. Perhaps they found more luxurious en suite accommodation elsewhere.

Adopting a slower timescale

I have also had badgers, foxes, hawks and squirrels in the garden even when living in the centre of London, and encountered my first opossums tap-dancing on the roof of my motel room in New England as they played tag around the neon sign. Patience is the key to observing wildlife in the garden, parks or animal-conservation areas. However, this is quite a hard lesson, accustomed as we are to the fast-fix, frantic modern world.

We cannot expect a deer to bound up towards a hide in the forest after two minutes because we want to see one – although I still secretly do. But after those seemingly endless periods of doing nothing except being still and quiet, comes the reward: a magnificent stag sharing a moment of his life as he stares at us before tossing his antlers, pawing the ground with his hooves and galloping out of sight.

At other times we may catch an unexpected glimpse of a smaller, less dramatic but no less wondrous bird or animal, such as a mouse cleaning its whiskers behind the garden shed or the first flight from the nest of young blackbirds in the eaves.

Forming a relationship with wildlife

When children can see realistic simulations of dinosaurs on television and videos of exotic creatures in the jungle, they may at first not understand the true wonder of squirrels in the park, or a hedgehog emerging from a pile of leaves, or a spider sitting in the centre of its jewelled web at dawn. But what can be more amazing than to have a badger, the size of a dog, living entirely wild in a copse behind a row of houses, coming and going at will, or a family of rabbits hopping across a city park at sunset?

WELCOMING WILDLIFE INTO YOUR WORLD

There are many ways you can encourage wildlife to be a part of your world:

- Begin by having a bird table or, if you live in an apartment, try hanging a tray from the balcony or window. Suddenly your garden will be filled with life, as birds swoop and dive, chatter and fight as they feed.

- Buy squirrel feeders, bat boxes and wooden hedgehog houses even if you have not sighted any of those animals in your garden, and leave a variety of nuts, seeds and berries inside each.

- Go to sanctuaries dedicated to conserving indigenous wildlife, where owls, otters, beavers, harvest mice and foxes live in large wild areas and it is the visitors who are behind glass. The animals have the option whether or not to appear. If you regularly visit the same sanctuary over a number of months you will see most of the species. Children love guessing which creatures will be out and which will be hiding.

- Visit places where you know there is wildlife, perhaps at particular seasons or at different times of the day. Some castles and parklands have herds of deer or squirrel woods, and urban parks are full of rabbits and other wildlife after dusk.

- The best times to see animals and birds in the wild are early morning and evening, and, for nocturnal creatures, after dark. Wildlife centres throughout the world offer night-time walks or studies. Many animal and bird conservation parks also have night houses where you can walk through a dimly lit area and observe the animals through a two-way shaded mirror so that they are unaware of your presence. The best centres have unobtrusive cameras into natural underground sets and burrows.

- Leave areas of untended undergrowth in your garden, especially near perimeter fences, to encourage small creatures to burrow and dig. A wildlife pond will attract frogs and dragonflies. Create herb beds of fast-spreading herbs, such as parsley and mint, to provide food for the small creatures.

- At weekends go camping or rent a caravan, camper van or wooden chalet in a forest, by a lake or in a national park. In New Zealand there is an excellent system of huts in which you can stay on long wilderness treks.

- Choose a quiet site and sit quietly just before dawn – when you will be rewarded by the dawn chorus – and at twilight.

EXPANDING THE HORIZONS

You can also use holidays in other places to get to know their local wildlife. For example, ten minutes from Los Angeles airport, at Marina del Rey, pelicans fly gracefully in formation and then settle like gossipy old women on the boats and the boardwalk as sunset floods the sky; in Giza, along the freeway from Cairo, the chattering carpet of ibis birds peck the growing crops on the green strips on either side of the irrigation canals, as they have done for thousands of years, while cars and buses whizz by only metres away; near Stockholm you can sit on the balcony of an apartment block or hotel and watch curious moose chewing the perimeter fence.

Uɴᴅᴇʀꜱᴛᴀɴᴅɪɴɢ ᴛʜᴇ ꜱɪɢɴɪꜰɪᴄᴀɴᴄᴇ ᴏꜰ ᴡɪʟᴅʟɪꜰᴇ ᴇɴᴄᴏᴜɴᴛᴇʀꜱ

In Native North America and among the Australian Aboriginals, wild animals are regarded as wise teachers. An adolescent would spend time in the wilderness during which time a particular bird or animal would come close and be adopted as the young person's totem or special creature that could bring them power and wisdom. We, too, can learn from wild animals and birds. On pages 181–7 I have suggested particular qualities that both homely creatures and more exotic wildlife can offer us psychologically and psychically to bring out the same strengths within ourselves (see also Chapter 11).

By watching birds in the same place regularly we can begin to discern individual personalities and may find that our special blackbird seems to appear at a time when we feel sad or anxious. Our special creatures may also appear at an unusual time in an unusual setting or in a recurring dream over several consecutive nights almost as a sign. One example of how wildlife can cast sudden meaning on events in our own lives was described by *Sunday Telegraph* columnist Christopher Booker, with whom I corresponded some years ago:

> For as long as I can remember, every year on my birthday, which falls in October, my dear mother recalled that she heard a blackbird singing in the garden the moment before I entered the world at 6.30 in the morning. Every year for at least 30 years I respectfully informed her that it could not have been a blackbird singing in October. It must have been a robin.
>
> Two weeks ago, my mother died, and on Wednesday last, I had the sad task of placing her ashes in the earth in a Dorset country churchyard. At that moment, two birds began to sing very loudly a few yards from her grave. One was a robin; the other was a blackbird. I hope she was able to share the joke; perhaps she arranged it. As I lowered the ashes into the ground and heard both robin

and blackbird striking up together, I had a smile on my face.

This significance can be dismissed as coincidence, but it does seem part of an underlying interconnected web of meaning through which we make sense of our worlds – and sometimes draw reassurance that life is not entirely random. You, too, can work informally with the energies of wild creatures to connect with this web of meaning. Decide what a number of creatures that share your environment mean to you – up to 20 birds and indigenous wild animals will work well. If you see one at an unusual place or time or during a dream and then afterwards in reality, you will know that the unconscious mind is trying to tell you something (see Appendix 5 for suggested meanings).

Unlike pets, creatures in the garden are unpredictable and may disappear for days or weeks without warning, so their sudden appearance can be used as a psychological marker. Let me tell you about Maggie's experience: Maggie lives in a town in the north of England and is a single parent in her forties. Her special birds are white herons with their huge white and grey wings. Herons can live in the centre of towns and may be seen fishing in canals or urban rivers as well as over marshes, lakes and near the ocean. Maggie has visited their wildlife habitats many times and draws strength from them, but she had always wanted to see one in her garden. This is what she told me:

> On the morning my 18-year-old only son, Joe, was due to set off backpacking round Europe, I was very worried about him going and knew I would miss him very much. I woke up early and, because I could not settle, went to the living room, which has a big picture window on to the garden. Standing in the centre of the grass was a beautiful white heron. When it saw me, it looked straight at me, expanded its wings and for a glorious moment seemed to connect with me; then it flapped its wings and flew off over the rooftops.
>
> Instantly I understood: I realised at that moment

that I needed to let Joe go and to trust that when he is ready he will return. Joe has been very happy in his travels and has mailed me many times. I have not seen the heron since but I know that he and Joe will come back safely in their own time.

For Maggie, the heron confirmed the rightness of giving her blessing to Joe's travels so he could fly freely without guilt at leaving her alone. Because the creature was a bird of flight that chose to visit her garden on that special day, the experience assumed psychological and psychical significance.

WORKING WITH YOUR SPECIAL WILDLIFE

This is a simple method for working with animals that seem to have meaning for you:

1 Make a list of any number of wild birds and animals the appearance of which brings you pleasure or that seem to appear at particularly significant times in your life. You might like to use a loose-leaf folder or keep a computer folder for these records. Note down the strengths the creatures seem to offer. Leave a page or so for each one (see Appendix 5).

2 Once you start a list, you may notice that the frequency of appearances increases or that you become aware of the powers of other creatures you had not noticed before.

3 As you build up your personal list over the months, you can collect feathers or charms in silver or crystal or tiny ceramic models of your favourite creatures, or you can download images from the Internet (this is allowed for non-commercial purposes) to stick on to small cards and laminate.

4 Read the folklore and myths about your favourite creatures in books or on-line so that you will understand

more about the qualities each species offers. You will usually find that the legends confirm your own ideas.

5 Then when you need a particular strength you can sleep with your image or charm by your bedside or hold the image or photograph between your hands and allow its energies to flow into you.

6 Carry symbols with you when you need their strengths during the day. You can carry, for example, a tiny crafted wooden fox in a small fabric bag in your pocket or briefcase when you are attending a confrontational and difficult meeting at work. This will help you to be aware of the undercurrents and to protect you when you know there may be underhand dealings.

HEALING URBAN WILDLIFE

Sometimes we may find a wild creature that has been injured, and suddenly its well-being is placed in our hands. Healing wild creatures can be more difficult than pets because of their natural fear of humans. But I have found some quite remarkable examples. Ray, who lives in London, told me:

> I was running a retail cycle shop, and every Saturday evening my wife and I would go to an Indian restaurant in Lewisham High Road to talk over the week. At that time the vast Thamesmead Estate in Essex was being built. My wife would often say as we went past it on the way home, 'Let's go and see how the estate is getting on.' My reply was always the same because I was tired after a hard week, 'I'm not going down that dirt track to look at a building site.'
>
> One evening, however, as we drove past the turning, I slammed on the brakes and reversed so that we could drive down the site. I stopped the car by some wasteland where poppies were growing. My wife said, 'Let's pick some', and for some reason I was compelled to get out of the car and go over to the second group of poppies. In the

centre of the poppies was a sparrow with its feet stuck in molten tar. There was no way I could extricate the bird without pulling off his feet, so I got out my pocket knife and cut a circle around the tar, leaving the bird attached. The bird did not struggle at all, and obviously it had not struggled previously otherwise it would have ripped off its feet. It was as though it was waiting for me.

I took the bird back to my workshop, as the only thing I could try was using solvent. It took three hours to finish the task and all the time the bird stood there patiently. It was eleven o'clock at night by the time I finished. Although I had been careful, the solvent got on to the bird's feathers, and by the time I had finished it was utterly lifeless, motionless and unrecognisable as a bird. It looked like a wet cigarette. It was soaked in solvent and overwhelmed by the fumes. But I had had no alternative other than to try to help, as I could not have left it attached to the tar to be attacked by vandals, killed by an animal or to starve to death. I was amazed it had not died of shock after its ordeal.

I placed the body on newspaper and laid it on the floor. As a hopeless gesture I crumbled a stale roll on to the paper and put some water in a dish nearby. Its heart was still beating faintly, showing through the white skin beneath its matted feathers. I locked the workshop and went home. The workshop had no holes in it and was empty of life apart from the bird.

The next morning I was anxious to bury the bird, as the incident had troubled me. When I opened the door, the body was no longer on the newspaper, but the bird was sitting perched on the vice, its feathers bright and fluffy. It was completely healed and cocked its head. I opened the two big doors. The bird looked at me, flew off and perched on the fence opposite. Then it looked back once before swooping off into the sky, completely restored. I am convinced that it was a sign that I was being watched over and blessed and the bird had been healed – but not by me.

BECOMING A HEALER OF WILD CREATURES

Such incidents are a powerful testimony to the healing powers that we possess when we have compassion for an animal or bird that is not a pet. Like Ray above, some people are naturally gifted. On page 98 I mentioned asking for help in our own healing work from angels who were associated with animals. Two saints have remained icons of all that is best in the relationship between humans and local wildlife; they are St Francis and St Blaise, and people have sought their help for wild animals over hundreds of years. If you find a sick or injured wild creature you can ask for healing through the intercession of one of these animal patron saints, whether you care for the creature yourself or seek the help of an animal or bird rescue organisation.

St Francis, patron saint of animals and birds

The most famous carer of wild creatures was St Francis of Assisi who, it is said, established the first Christmas crib. He created it in 1223 in a cave in the hills of Grecchia, using real animals so that people could understand the true significance of Christmas.

Born to a wealthy family *c.* 1181, Francis became a wandering preacher and, in 1209, founded the Franciscans. He was famed for the way wild animals and birds would come close to him and be silent as he spoke and prayed, and he healed many of them. They were said to gather round him like a human congregation. The first environmentalist, Francis wrote a prayer that is still used at services of animal healing and blessings held at a number of churches today. You may find it helpful to say this prayer when you are sending healing to a wild creature or an endangered species:

> *God Our Heavenly Father,*
> *By our own fault we have lost the beautiful relationship*
> *which we once had with all your creation. Give us the*
> *grace to see all animals as gifts from You and to treat them*

*with respect, for they are Your creation. We pray for all
animals that are suffering as a result of our neglect. May
the order You originally established be once again restored
to the whole world through the intercession of the Glorious
Virgin Mary, the prayers of St Francis and the merits of
Your Son, Our Lord Jesus Christ.
Amen*

St Blaise

The second patron saint for animals is St Blaise. He is an even
earlier saint associated with animals, and he can also form a
focus for your own healing world with wildlife. Blaise was an
Armenian bishop who, when persecutions began, withdrew
to become a hermit in a cave where he became famed for healing animals. Sick animals, both gentle and fierce, would come
to his cave, waiting patiently until he finished his prayers;
even the fiercest became docile as they gathered round to hear
him speak. The story tells that when he was arrested in
316 CE, he was found by the Roman Emperor's hunters surrounded by wild animals of all kinds.

HEALING LOCAL WILDLIFE

On page 97 I mentioned how Margaret used a healing book in
which she wrote the names of people and animals who needed
help. You can create one of these, listing not only any sick pets
you know but also indigenous species of animals, birds, reptiles, insects or butterflies and any injured wild creatures you
find or hear of. You can even list particular projects you would
like to see preserved. You can use the book to send healing to
wildlife affected by disasters; for example, by oil slicks or
chemical spillage in different areas. The numbers of creatures
to record in your book will increase as though by magic once
you focus on animal healing, and you will not be able to open
the newspaper or talk to a neighbour without learning of a
new case. This may be because we become more aware or it

may be that the more positive messages we send out the more needy creatures will come to our attention.

As with animal symbols, if you use a loose-leafed folder, you can attach any newspaper cuttings or pictures you have of a threatened species and/or endangered wildlife area as well as any individual creatures that have been adversely affected by a particular occurrence, such as a local hedgerow being cut down. The following steps will show you how to send healing:

1 When you have time, perhaps once a week during the evening, light a white or pink candle and read aloud or in your mind each entry, adding a private blessing.

2 You may then decide to choose one creature or cause that is close to your heart or that has been in the news, and visualise the creature well and safe.

3 Blow out the candle and send the light to your chosen cause(s).

4 If anyone in your family finds an injured or weak creature, you can carry out this simple ceremony either to aid its recovery or to bring a gentle death. This can be immensely comforting for small children who easily link with the creature's distress. (Remember, never leave a burning candle unattended.)

If you have time, make a small practical gesture to help your weekly chosen cause or species, as this will extend the influence of your blessings. If every animal and bird lover spent a few minutes focusing on the personal causes dear to his or her heart, we really could increase the positive and practical energies for preservation and conservation.

In the next chapter, I will talk about more exotic animals, the ways they offer healing to humans and also how we can use their energies to give us strength.

11 | Encountering exotic creatures

THIS CHAPTER IS ABOUT the more unusual wild creatures that live in their natural habitats or in conservation areas or parks. They are conventionally regarded as hostile or indifferent to humans, because they are fierce or because they keep a distance from people. Even people who care for wild animals in animal parks are taught to be wary, as injuries and fatalities among keepers have occurred a number of times over the past few years in zoos around the world. But in spite of this, even the fiercest creatures can be friends to humans. There is some overlap between this chapter and the previous one because whether an animal is exotic will depend to some extent on your location; for example, you may have dolphins regularly swimming in your local bay or monkeys raiding your garden for fruit.

THE ALTRUISM OF WILD ANIMALS

There are many attested cases of fierce creatures showing kindness and protectiveness towards humans. A recent example that made the headlines was of Binti Jua, an eight-year-old western lowland gorilla that, on 16 August 1996, rescued a three-year-old boy when he climbed a railing and fell 5½ metres (18 feet) on to concrete inside the gorilla enclosure at Brookfield Zoo in Chicago. There were seven gorillas in the enclosure at the time, but Binti at once made sure the child was not harmed. Binti rocked the unconscious boy in her arms and carried him to safety to one of the keeper's entrances to the enclosure, while her own 17-month-old baby daughter, Koola, rode on her back. Binti kept the other gorillas away until the child could be removed.

Even more surprising is that a male gorilla, Jambo, during the summer of 1986 demonstrated similar gentleness when Lee, a five-year-old boy, slipped and fell into the open-air gorilla compound at Jersey's Wildlife Preservation Trust on the Channel Islands. As Lee lay unconscious with a fractured skull and arm, Jambo, a huge silverback gorilla, stroked the boy's back and kept the other curious gorillas at a safe distance while keepers rescued the child.

UNDERSTANDING WILD ANIMALS

Both the above zoos have an excellent record for animal conservation and there are other similar centres of excellence around the world, such as wildcat and monkey sanctuaries, wolf centres and gigantic sea-world aquaria. Also, there are conservation areas in the animals' native habitats where it is possible to see wild animals living in natural but protected conditions.

Check out any zoos or animal centres in your own area to make sure that you are happy with the conditions there, and you may wish to support their work practically or financially; often you can adopt an exotic creature for less than the cost of a day pass to a theme park. When you holiday abroad, use the Internet and guidebooks for the region to obtain impartial opinions from visitors and conservation organisations about the quality of centres where animals are kept.

If you are concerned about animal welfare, you should act upon it, but always make sure you understand the circumstances first; for example, if you are concerned about the space an animal is allotted in any wildlife park, ask those who care for the animals. Sometimes a creature that has been rescued from bad conditions wants to stay in a small area to begin with and may only gradually cope with more freedom in a larger area. Or a park may be desperately trying to improve conditions but lacks resources to do so; boycotting it may not be as helpful as asking how you can help with positive publicity, and so on. Usually those who care for wild animals really do care – the keepers in Kabul zoo worked without wages and did all they could to feed and keep the creatures safe during the conflicts in Afghanistan.

A number of animal lovers believe animals should not be kept in captivity at all, but sadly for some species it is their only chance of survival. Some creatures are released again into the wilderness; unfortunately, some of them fall prey to poachers after their release.

TALKING TO THE ANIMALS

You may already have a favourite large or small exotic creature, such as the endangered Madagascan lemur, or a nocturnal animal like a marmoset or the desert fennec fox. If not, visit a good sanctuary; if you go several times, you will soon identify *your* creature, who will unexpectedly move towards the enclosure fence and then watch you, motionless. For a few seconds you may link with the creature and perhaps share a moment of wordless communication.

FIERCE CREATURES THAT REAR HUMAN BABIES

It is said that no creature is fiercer in defence of her young than a mother wolf. This protectiveness towards young extends to human infants. The most well-known wolf-mother legend is that of Romulus and Remus – the founders of Rome. According to myth they were the sons of the god of war, Mars, and Rhea Silvia, one of the vestal virgins, who was killed because she was falsely accused of breaking her vows of chastity. Her sons were left in the wilderness to die. But the infants were suckled by a she-wolf.

Myths such as this could be based on fact, for throughout the ages there have been real cases of the adoption of humans by animals. The classic source is Lucien Malson's *Les Enfants Sauvages*, translated into English by E. Fawcett and others in 1972. He listed 53 wild children in different countries since 1344. Several more cases have been discovered since the book's original publication in Paris in 1964. By far the majority of wild children were suckled and/or protected by wolves.

One of the most famous cases was that from Midnapore in India. In 1920 the Reverend A. Singh became intrigued after locals described two malevolent *manush-baghas* – small ghostly creatures with blazing eyes – that haunted villagers from the forests near Denganalia. A female wolf always accompanied the creatures, and it was discovered that their lair was located in an abandoned ant heap. The Reverend Singh decided after two fleeting glimpses that the ghosts were human children running on all fours. He arranged for local tribesmen to dig the lair out, and on 17 October the ant beaters and diggers surrounded the heap. Two wolves ran out as soon as the digging started and broke through the cordon. A third wolf, a female, appeared and, according to Singh's journal, instead of running away, made for the diggers, scattering them to all sides before diving back into the hole.

The female wolf made a second charge at the diggers, only this time the bowmen were standing by at close range. Before the Reverend Singh could stop them, they loosed off their arrows and killed the mother. The ant heap was opened and the two children found huddled in a ball with two wolf cubs. After a fierce struggle they were separated. The two wolf cubs were sold and the two children were taken to Midnapore Orphanage. The youngest, aged three at the time of her discovery, died within a year. The second girl, who was about five years old and who they named Kamala, lived for nine years, eventually learning to stand upright, to eat by hand and speak about 30 words of English, the language used by the missionaries.

Similar cases involving wild dogs have been reported very recently. In November 1996, a newborn baby abandoned in sub-zero temperatures in the Romanian capital Bucharest was saved by a pack of wild dogs. Two dogs stood guard over the tiny bundle while the barking of two others attracted patrolling police officers. The boy was found covered in fallen leaves and with the remains of his umbilical cord and placenta attached. It was thought that a dog had licked the baby's body clean. The child was adopted by one of the policemen.

Such altruism suggests once again that perhaps even the fiercest creatures are capable of higher feelings. In societies where we do not need to hunt to survive we need to rethink our attitudes towards those wild creatures that we may traditionally have believed to be the enemies of humans.

CONNECTING WITH THE POWER OF THE WILD

As you become more familiar with a number of wild creatures, you may discover that one or two become your special power animals, the qualities of which you especially admire. You may also find that they may appear to you in dreams or their images appear in your mind's eye unexpectedly at times of significance in your life (see also page 144). You may decide to pick a fierce predator for those times when you need courage, and perhaps a bird that can fly away or a smaller creature that can burrow away from danger when flight is more prudent than fight.

In Appendix 5 I have listed a number of fierce creatures, the qualities of which may be useful at different stages in your life. As with indigenous wildlife, the more you can find out about the myths and legends surrounding your chosen creature, the more you will understand them.

ADDING TO YOUR STORE OF ANIMAL STRENGTHS

You may like to collect ten or 20 creatures whose strengths you can store to be used when needed. To gain inspiration, you can watch videos of wild creatures in their natural habitats, or you can download images from the Internet. In time you will have a number of core creatures to add to your indigenous wildlife, animal and bird list, the symbols of which you can collect and carry with you.

Play CDs of different wild animal sounds, birdcalls, and rainforest and ocean sounds when you are sitting quietly in the evening. By absorbing the powers of different wild creatures psychologically and spiritually, you can feel more courageous and confident in your everyday world: you can be the mother wolf protecting her young against playground bullying by insisting an unwilling school takes action; you can walk stealthily like a panther through the office jungle, occasionally revealing your teeth and claws so that critical bosses and jealous colleagues back off. Conversely you can lower your profile at times when you want or need to remain unnoticed; for example, if you find yourself in a dark, lonely place or are feeling scared home alone at night.

The following is a method that I have used successfully many times and taught with instant success even to people who have never worked with animal powers before:

1 Imagine your power animal or bird to be full human size in front of you and listen in your mind to its breathing, whether slow and deep or tiny panting breaths. If you have watched videos of your creature you may be familiar with the breath pattern or there may be audio clips on the Internet for you to refer to.

2 Match the creature's breathing either aloud if you are alone, or in your mind.

3 As you continue to breathe, imagine the creature's strengths flowing into your own body; on your out breaths, picture your own fears and sense of weakness

and any buried anger flowing from you, perhaps as rays of dark-coloured light or mist.

4 Continue to inhale and exhale more quietly but still rhythmically. While you are doing this, visualise the current scene – whether it is a lonely street or an abusive stranger – through the eyes of your power creature. As you move, feel the paws padding beneath you, the mighty strides or the almost imperceptible scurry to safety.

5 When you are ready, shake your fingers and feet and step out of your power creature, thanking him or her for safe passage.

With practice you will be able to step within your animals' power and protection just by picturing them.

DOLPHINS AND WHALES – SPIRITUAL HEALING POWERS

These are the most magical of all wild creatures, and the dolphin especially has become a symbol of human healing and protection. In mythology, dolphins have been regarded as very special. A number of the ancient sea goddesses adopted this most intelligent and sensitive of creatures for their icon, including Aphrodite, the Greek goddess of love, the Egyptian goddess Isis, and Stella Maris, star and goddess of the sea. In Maori mythology, two of the sea gods take the form of whales and it is believed that they can occasionally be seen along the eastern coast of New Zealand's South Island, the island they are said to have created.

Traditionally, dolphins have been friends to humans; for example, between 1888 and 1912, a rare white Risso's dolphin that was called Pelorus Jack safely guided steamers through the treacherous waters of Pelorus Sound, off South Island, New Zealand. In 1904 a law was passed to protect him after someone tried to shoot him from one of the steamers.

Dolphins as lifesavers

Throughout history dolphins have been lifesavers. The Greek historian Herodotus recounted how a dolphin saved the harpist Arion after Corinthian sailors had thrown him overboard from the ship on which he was travelling. The dolphin carried Arion to Taenarus, his destination. There are also countless stories of dolphin rescues in recent times; for example, the case of Doris who, in April 1997, was snorkelling off Garvies Beach near Durban in South Africa when she ran into difficulties and was in danger of drowning. Five dolphins supported her and took her to shore.

In January 1998 three teenage boys were surfing near a school of dolphins off Halftide Beach in New South Wales, Australia. One of the boys, Adam, was attacked by a shark. The dolphins protected the boy by driving off the shark and then supporting his body back to shore.

The intelligence of dolphins is well attested. But there also seems to be evidence that they experience higher emotions associated with humans, such as altruism and concern for others who may be in danger, even for those who are not part of their immediate kin or species. Dolphins are sometimes kept in oceanariums, and in these circumstances we should remember how privileged we are to experience close contact with them in this way, and that their needs must predominate over commercial considerations.

Dolphins as healers

Over the past 20 years we have discovered that dolphins have great healing powers that can benefit humans. They are especially helpful to autistic children and those with cerebral palsy and other forms of brain damage. David Nathanson, a clinical psychologist living in Florida, has used dolphin therapy with Down's syndrome children during the 1970s. He discovered that children with learning disabilities who swam with dolphins learned up to four times faster and remembered much more when they were taught immediately after swimming with the dolphins than those taught similar material in the usual classroom situation. By the 1980s a dolphin centre had been established in Key West, Florida, and since then it has helped children from all over the world.

A remarkable example of dolphin healing is that of Nikki from Weston-super-Mare, in Somerset, England. Nikki technically died at birth, and although doctors were able to revive him, he suffered minor brain damage. At eight years old, Nikki had never spoken, in spite of the fact that neurological experts found no physical reason, since his hearing was normal and his vocal cords were fully functional. He communicated only by grunting for 'yes' and 'no' and through facial gestures, in spite of intensive therapy.

In 1998 his mother, Tabitha, raised the money to take Nikki to the Human Dolphin Therapy Center at the Sea-Aquarium in Miami, which uses 40-minute swimming sessions with trained dolphins, as well as intensive conventional therapies.

Although Nikki was initially apprehensive, his mother reported that before long he was happily playing with the dolphins. She told newspaper reporters:

> On the third day, Nikki was swimming in the dolphin enclosure. We hadn't been there for long when Nikki was told to get out of the water at the end of the session … Nikki must have thought he wasn't going to be allowed to go swimming with the dolphins again because he suddenly pointed at the water and said 'in'. He was telling us he wanted to get back into the water … I have hoped for years to hear Nikki speak.

Dolphin therapies are so successful that they are now used worldwide, and in November 1993 a dolphin therapy centre was opened in Japan in the grounds of the Myoren-Ji Temple in Kyoto that was founded centuries earlier, in 1294.

How dolphin healing works

Dolphin healing does work, not only with children but also with seriously depressed adults. One theory for its success is that the sound waves produced by dolphins brings healing to body tissue and cells. However, others believe that the dolphins work on an emotional and spiritual level.

Bringing dolphins into the everyday world

If dolphin healing is of a spiritual rather than physical nature then its beneficial effects can be felt even without the dolphin's presence. David Nathanson and other researchers are now trying to create a virtual dolphin experience, using video and computer technology to benefit children who cannot travel to a dolphin centre either because they cannot afford to or because they are not physically able to. Heidi, who lives in Holland, explained:

> My son is autistic; he does not use language to communicate, but uses love – heart contact instead of head contact. During his life I have been searching for many ways to find appropriate therapies that will help to make his life pleasant and easier, in his own way.
>
> One day I read a book by a lady who worked with dolphins. She had developed a special way to communicate with them ... she started to work with autistic people and people with learning and physical disabilities. She brought them into contact with the dolphins and developed a very beneficial therapy. I became curious and wanted to do the same for my son.
>
> I started to look for a way, and from that moment on, dolphins swam into my life. I started to work with their energy, with the sounds, music and images, etc. It helped me and it helped my son. I painted lively dolphins on his wall, and one day I noticed their spirit was really there. They helped me to heal or calm my son when he was upset or could not sleep.
>
> With my family and friends I collected money to be able to give my son healing therapy with real dolphins. He has had some sessions already and it has benefited him so much.

Heidi herself had an unexpected encounter with a wild dolphin when she was on the Egyptian coast:

> I went into the water and suddenly a dolphin came straight up to me, stretched itself out of the water and looked right into my eyes. I was overwhelmed by powerful feelings of acceptance, love and recognition. This wise being knew me by one look from his deep dark eye, he came especially to meet me, to contact me. I cannot describe what I felt, but I cried and laughed at the same time, and I will never forget that look.

Dolphin healing at home for stress and anxiety

Although we cannot all swim with dolphins or see them in the wild, we can recreate something of the joy. Like Heidi, you can use dolphin images, especially in the bathroom, to help you to relax. Listen to dolphin music by the light of a blue candle, holding in each hand an aquamarine or jade crystal. Crystals in the water will increase the energy flow. The following method is one I use when I am depressed or anxious and is excellent for curing insomnia:

1 Light turquoise-coloured candles in your bathroom.

2 Use blue or green bath salts (not foam) containing lavender or kelp, if possible.

3 Drop one tiny aquamarine or jade crystal into each pool of light in the bath. As these are water crystals they will help to invoke the power of the sea.

4 Play your dolphin CD either in a waterproof portable battery player or by using special speakers in the bathroom (it is well worth being wired in safely, as music when bathing can be so uplifting after a stressful day).

5 Make sure the water is warm.

6 Close your eyes and visualise the dolphins swimming towards you.

7 Reach out and touch them in your mind's vision. Ride on their backs through the white-capped waves, and as they swim away, see them carrying away any pain or tension.

If there is a floatation tank near to your home, you could take your dolphin tape along for a truly magical experience. Floatation tanks may be found in a number of alternative health centres or even health clubs or spas. The tanks are very safe even for non-swimmers, because the saline water is so concentrated that even if you fall asleep (which most people do) you cannot sink. You lie in semi-darkness, and sessions last for about an hour; if you ask the therapists to play your dolphin music into the floatation room during the session you may find that imaginary dolphins float into your consciousness unbidden. Because you are in a deeply relaxed state you may begin to understand something of their wisdom, perhaps telepathically.

Dolphin tapes are also excellent for playing in the bedrooms of restless children and work well with insomniacs of all ages. They also soothe hyperactivity naturally and make good background music while children play.

In the final sections of the book, I have drawn together a variety of useful material: crystals, herbs and flower essences that are especially good for healing animals; the strengths different animals contain; and, finally, a list of names with their meanings that have been given to creatures of all kinds – you might find these useful if you are choosing a pet.

Appendix 1
Crystals
and animals

The following crystals are good for protective and healing work with animals and birds of all kinds:

Amber
Colours: yellow, golden orange or a rich golden brown often containing fossilised insects or tiny plants
Good for promoting self-healing and strengthening the immune system. It is excellent for older animals or those with chronic conditions, such as painful joints or bones. Helps to counter the effects of external noise and pollution and is a gentle energiser in pet water.

Amethyst
Colours: shades of purple, from pale to deep, sometimes with white
Another all-healer, amethyst is especially useful for an animal that has suffered previous abuse or neglect; good for stomach problems and all difficulties with eating (useful when putting a pet on a diet), as well as travel sickness. Soak an amethyst in pet water to calm hyperactivity and aggressiveness, and to prevent destructive behaviour; for example, excessive barking in a dog or when a bird pulls out its feathers. Amethyst is effective against fleas, mites and ticks.

Angelite
Colours: pale or mid blue
This is the stone for all guide and assistance animals and those who live with a chronically sick or depressed owner. A

natural healer for chest and fluid problems, throat and gland problems, ear or eye inflammation and to assist weight loss. It also encourages strong-willed animals to be more docile.

Aquamarine
Colours: clear light blue or blue green
Aquamarine is good for problems with teeth and gums, bladder and kidney disorders in animals and in relieving shock and trauma. Aquamarines can maintain the health of fish and marine life, especially tropical, if placed in a tank or pond.

Banded agate
Colours: use brown, pink and fawn banded agates
An all-healer, banded agate is good for calming any creature and stabilising emotions and health. It is especially helpful for skin and stomach disorders.

Bloodstone
Colours: dark green with red spots and occasionally white patches
Bloodstones are effective for all problems with the blood, for increasing healing after an operation, in labour, especially for first-time mother animals and to ease problems when a female is on heat. Attach a small bloodstone to a pet collar to help animals withstand bullies.

Blue calcite
Colours: pale to mid blue, like water ice
Good for teeth and bones, fevers and wounds. Blue calcite protects animals and birds from being stolen, and calms bad-tempered pets. Especially healing for birds of all kinds and cold-water fish.

Blue lace agate
Colours: pale blue, sometimes brighter blue with white lace threads
The most peaceful of stones, blue lace agate will calm even

the noisiest or most hyperactive animal or bird and is good to have in the home if you have more than one pet; soothes throat and gland problems, allergies and bone disorders. Very effective in quietening yowling cats, howling dogs or screeching birds.

Carnelian
Colours: orange to blood red
Good for female animals to increase fertility and to ease them through pregnancy and birth; gives energy to all animals, especially large ones. Place one in the mane or bridle of a horse to make training easier. Carnelian encourages timid, small animals, such as guinea pigs, to become more sociable. It is also the stone of goldfish and exotic birds, such as parrots and parakeets.

Cat's eye
Colours: orangey brown, yellow, golden, orange or green; resembles a cat's eye
The stone can be used to maintain the health and well-being of all cats, especially pedigree ones. Attach one to collars of cats to protect them from harm after dark.

Dalmatian jasper
Colours: black spots on a fawn or cream background
The ultimate stone for healing dogs, Dalmatian jasper eases bowel problems in all animals; will increase the effect of any medical treatment, especially alternative methods using herbal and flower essence remedies. It strengthens telepathic communication with any animal and brings out the natural healing abilities of owners.

Desert rose
Colours: pale brown, it has a rough texture with glints of silver or pearl
Desert rose helps an animal to overcome viruses; good for skin disorders, relieving travel sickness and phobias. It is the crystal for lizards, snakes and small desert animals, such as

hamsters and guinea pigs. Also good for very old and sick creatures of all kinds.

Green fluorite
Colours: deep glass-like green
Green fluorite counters the pollution and stresses of urban life. It is good for healing wounds, alleviating rheumatism and arthritis in an animal and for hormonal problems. It also calms fears and phobias. Place green fluorite in a garden or window box to attract wildlife, especially birds, dragonflies and butterflies. Green fluorite helps animals to settle when out of their natural habitat.

Hawk's/falcon's eye
Colours: blue or green form of tiger's eye.
Hawk's eye relieves eye, spine, neck and leg problems and helps older animals to be more mobile. It protects all creatures during travel and when away from home; for example, an overnight stay at the vet. It is health-giving for all birds, both pets and wild birds, but especially hawks and birds of prey. The cat's eye form protects cats.

Jade
Colours: pale to dark green
One of the most healing stones for animals and, indeed, all creatures, jade promotes long life and health; it eases bladder and kidney problems, fluid retention, blood sugar imbalances, lung and eye problems, and bone and joint pain or stiffness. It is a natural calmer that will heal memories of abuse, neglect or trauma. It is also helpful for a creature giving birth and for the health of her young. Jade also protects animals, especially young ones, against malice and cruelty from strangers.

Leopardskin jasper/rhyolite
Colours: brown, grey or dark sand with close brown or black spots and swirls that resemble a leopard's skin
Leopardskin jasper will gradually increase good health and energy in an exhausted animal or one that has been very ill. It

is good for skin problems, infections, bites and stings. It is another cat stone that encourages telepathic communication with owners. Also used for the well-being of snakes and lizards.

Malachite
Colours: from emerald to grass green with black or occasionally pale green stripes, bands or swirls (often marked like a marble)

Malachite is protective for creatures who live in the centre of towns or in homes near radio masts, power stations or electricity pylons. It triggers the immune system, especially against chemical and technological pollutants. It also strengthens teeth and bones. Do not put in pet water, as some people believe the stone is slightly toxic if absorbed.

Manganocalcite/pink calcite
Colours: pink, usually pale

Manganocalcite and, indeed, all pink calcite relieve chronic conditions and help pain. It is especially useful for animals that were rejected by their mothers or had a traumatic early life; it will help animals from rescue centres to settle in their new homes.

Moonstone
Colours: white, cream, peach, pink, grey and occasionally blue

Moonstone encourages regular reproductive cycles in female animals. It links all pets to natural rhythms, especially lunar ones. Moonstone also relieves problems with fluids, bladder and kidneys. It is a crystal for all nocturnal creatures and especially cats to keep them safe at night, and it also calms neurotic animals.

Moss agate
Colours: colourless with a profusion of deep green tendrils; also pale blue or a deeper green with pale blue or white inclusions

Moss agate encourages the growth and regrowth of cells and tissues, speeds the healing of wounds and is restorative after an operation or long illness; it relieves infections, especially those of the skin, and helps prevent dehydration, especially in hot weather. Moss agate gives animals in towns a link with the natural world. Place moss agate in the garden to encourage wildlife and birds. It is also a stone for rabbits, tame and wild.

Obsidian
Colours: black; also a transparent kind called apache tear
Obsidian is a pain reliever and can help animals with poor circulation. It is excellent if an animal has been involved in an accident or has been attacked by another animal. The more transparent apache tear will comfort a very old or sick animal and, when the time comes, ease its passing. Use also to help a creature that has lost its mate or owner. Obsidian is very protective for animals in transit.

Rose quartz
Colours: pale to deep pink
Rose quartz is another stone that can be used for all kinds of pet healing: for heart conditions, sprains or to relieve pain; also to restore trust in animals or birds that have been cruelly treated, especially when very young. Rose quartz assists stray or rescue animals to settle into a new home, and protects pregnant animals and their young and encourages lactation. It also quietens hyperactive or aggressive animals.

Rutilated quartz
Colours: clear or dark quartz with golden-yellow mineral needles inside
Rutilated quartz relieves bronchial conditions in an animal, also allergies and skin complaints. It protects urban animals and is helpful for older animals. It also increases the charisma of creatures that are physically unlovely, and brings out altruistic tendencies in all pets.

Snowflake obsidian
Colours: black with white spots or flower shapes
Snowflake obsidian will improve circulation problems, and ease chronic pain and eye problems in all creatures. It is very healing for horses, especially those that have suffered trauma or are very highly strung. Snowflake obsidian protects all creatures against malice. It is also helpful for all nocturnal or cold-blooded creatures.

Sodalite
Colours: deep blue with white flecks of calcite
Sodalite is a stone to balance the hormone, fat and sugar levels. It calms all stressed creatures, and eases problems with ears, sinuses, mouth and glands. Sodalite soothes mother animals when their young are taken away after weaning, and also the young on their first nights alone. It also maintains the health of birds.

Tiger's eye
Colours: honey or golden-brown gleaming bands
Tiger's eye is an energiser for exhausted or weak animals, filling creatures with a sense of well-being. It assists digestive disorders, ulcers and abrasions of all kinds, as well as rheumatic joints and bones. Tiger's eye gives timid animals courage without aggressiveness. It is also good for reducing the dominance of an animal that has become a domestic tyrant either with humans or other pets.

Tree agate
Colours: white with green, tree-like inclusions
Tree agate relieves bone, vein, capillary and skin problems. It encourages growth, especially of fur. Tree agate is good for connecting urban animals with nature and for all wildlife that lives in your garden, especially tree-dwelling creatures, such as squirrels and birds.

Turquoise

Colours: light blue/blue-green

Turquoise is the most protective of animal crystals, guarding against toxicity, pollution, malice and danger, especially when travelling. It is traditionally worn on collars and bridles, or attached to mirrors in birdcages and to small animal cages, to cast a barrier of security around the animal and to prevent it from straying or getting lost.

Appendix 2
Herbal remedies
for pets

The following are herbs that are used both by professionals and pet owners to increase the health and well-being of their animals. Always read labels carefully, and if in doubt or if a pet does not recover quickly, consult a vet or homeopathic animal practitioner. The weight of the pet is usually a deciding factor for the dosage. However, what suits one species may not always be right for another, so check labels for suitability for your species of pet as well as for the correct dosage.

Remember, some herbs are unsuitable for pregnant animals or nursing mothers (even a seemingly harmless culinary herb, such as parsley) so do check the labels, or refer to a good herb book or ask the vet. The following herbs are some of the most common ones to avoid during an animal's pregnancy: aloe vera, angelica, anise, autumn crocus, barberry, basil, bay, black cohosh, caraway, cayenne, elder, fennel, feverfew, golden seal, hyssop, juniper, male fern, mandrake, parsley, pennyroyal, poke rosemary, root, rue, sage, southernwood, tansy, tarragon, thuja, thyme, wintergreen, wormwood and yarrow.

The following list is a selection of the most frequently used herbs:

Alfalfa
Internally: a good source of vitamins and minerals. It helps the liver and kidneys, relieves rheumatism, arthritis and allergies. Alfalfa is a detoxifier for birds as well as animals; it restores the appetite in convalescing or chronically sick pets and improves freshness of breath.

Aloe vera

Internally: it is good for arthritis, allergies, digestive disorders and fur balls in the stomach, yeast infections, and liver and kidney imbalances. Use the powdered form for cats.

Externally: the gel relieves minor burns, skin rashes and wounds. It also relieves skin irritation in birds that pluck their own feathers.

Arnica

Externally: infused arnica oil, or liniment, is good for broken bones, strains, sprains and bruises, shock and superficial cuts in larger animals, especially horses; not for deep cuts. Also used for arthritis and as pain relief.

Bee pollen

Internally: given regularly, bee pollen is believed to keep an animal young and to keep hormones balanced and soothe allergies and digestion. Bee pollen increases the self-healing powers of the body.

Black cohosh

Internally: balances hormones. Black cohosh is good for fertility in female animals. It also helps thyroid problems. It helps fur to regrow, and is very healing for animals that have been spayed.

Catnip

Internally: for all animals for digestive disorders, colds, flu and fevers.

Externally: sprinkled around the sitting area, it encourages vitality and well-being in cats.

Chamomile

Internally: this is a very gentle herb, for digestive disorders and internal parasites. It will help fight bacteria, colds and chest infections. It is also soothing against stress, and calms birds that have been badly frightened.

Externally: it can be used to treat skin problems, prevent wound infections, relieve painful sores and improve the condition of fur.

Very occasionally chamomile causes an allergic reaction so be careful to follow recommended doses.

Comfrey
Externally: comfrey is useful as a poultice for injured horses with broken legs; also for all strains, scratches and sprains. But do not use on deep cuts, as comfrey can encourage tissue to form over the wound before it heals deep down.

Dandelion
Internally: dandelion is helpful for liver and digestive problems, anaemia and arthritis, for kidneys and bladder problems, especially in horses. It is also useful to alleviate fluid retention and to detoxify the system.

Echinacea (purple cornflower)
Internally: echinacea stimulates the immune system and helps animals and birds to fight infections and viruses, including colds and flu, and also bacteria. It is good for glands, for recovery after illness or an operation and for the renewal of healthy tissue. Echinacea is also useful for skin allergies in birds.

Eyebright
Externally: good used as an eye wash for all pets' eye problems, such as inflammation; it is one of the best remedies for parrots with eye problems.

Garlic
Internally: good for getting rid of internal parasites, garlic also protects the liver from damage caused by modern pollution. It is a natural antibiotic that does not interfere with the body's own natural bacteria in the digestive tract, and is also effective against viruses. Good also for keeping down fat levels.

Use in moderation, for short periods and follow dosage strictly.

Ginger

Internally: in water, ginger prevents travel sickness in pets and is good for digestive disorders generally; it can also be used with larger birds.

Goldenseal

Internally: mixed with echinacea, it counters infections.
Externally: goldenseal can be used as an antiseptic to cleanse wounds – often combined with aloe vera.

Kelp (seaweed)

Internally: as powder or granules, kelp is a good source of iodine that helps to keep the thyroid healthy, as well as alleviating problems with glands, the metabolism, fur, teeth and for digestive disorders. It is naturally anti-fungal and anti-viral. Kelp is good for maintaining pet health, including birds.

Lavender

Externally: sprinkle lavender heads near bedding to deter fleas; place lavender oil or pots of lavender near to where pets sleep to calm a stressed pet.

Milk thistle

Internally: milk thistle helps with all liver problems; very safe for pets, including birds; for chronic skin conditions. It is excellent for restoring natural immunity and health after prolonged medical intervention.

Mint

Internally: fresh mint in early morning water or food prevents travel sickness, although it is not recommended for cats as some can react adversely. Mint is a natural digestive and breath freshener and it also restores a lost appetite.
Externally: keep fresh mint in a car with dogs or in a horse-box when making long journeys.

Nettles

Internally: an excellent diuretic, thus keeping bladder and kidneys healthy. Nettles also relieve anaemia, colds and allergies.

Parsley

Internally: a natural diuretic, parsley is therefore helpful for kidney and bladder problems and reducing incontinence in an old animal, for aiding digestion and for improving sweetness of breath. It contains natural oestrogen and so is good for females you would like to breed from (though should not be given in pregnancy) and also older female animals. Parsley builds up natural immunity.

Raspberry leaf

Internally: as with raspberry leaf for humans, this helps a pregnant animal and will stimulate milk production after the birth.

Slippery elm bark

Internally: slippery elm bark relieves diarrhoea and sickness and calms over-sensitive stomachs. It is also good for coughs and is excellent as a nutrient for weak animals whether old, very young or chronically ill.

Externally: slippery elm bark is helpful for skin complaints, wounds and inflammation of skin, burns and abscesses.

Tea tree oil

Externally: a drop of tea tree oil can be placed on a fungal infection, such as ringworm, or on a dry or inflamed patch (if you place a slice of cucumber on the affected area first this will cleanse it and also soothe the area); it is also an antiseptic, but keep away from eyes and genitals. Used as pet toothpaste, it improves the health of teeth and gums.

Thyme

Internally: aids digestion, colds and coughs and respiratory problems. Thyme is a powerful antiseptic, so is useful for wounds that will not heal. It is also used for digestive disorders, throat infections, coughs and respiratory problems, and relieves flatulence in pets. Thyme is especially useful for urban animals.

Yarrow

Internally: yarrow assists liver and bladder problems, and internal bleeding. Under expert supervision, yarrow is sometimes used for animals with diabetes. It also relieves infections, fever and diarrhoea.

Externally: yarrow will help wounds to heal, stop them becoming infected and relieve skin irritation.

NATURAL PEST CONTROL

Herbs really come into their own in alleviating the problem of parasites. With wall-to-wall carpeting and central heating, fleas can be a real problem for many pet owners all year round, but many people are nevertheless worried by the high chemical toxicity in some commercial flea collars and sprays. There are a number of pet-friendly methods you can use that will also not upset children or sensitive adults in the home who may be allergic to chemicals. Herbal flea collars and pet washes are available commercially.

You can add a few drops of eucalyptus, tea tree or lavender essential oil to the inside of an ordinary fabric pet collar weekly. Occasionally, when you bath an animal you can use an infusion (the strained liquid) in its bath. Use a small cup filled with any one, or a mixture, of the following herbs: fresh chopped rosemary, pennyroyal and lavender. Put these in a jug and add about 500 millilitres (17 fluid ounces) of boiling water. Leave the herbs to soak in the boiling water for about five minutes. Strain and discard the herbs. You can store the infusion in a sealed bottle and it will keep for about a week in the refrigerator. Add to a pet bath or apply to the fur and leave to dry. As well as controlling the fleas, you will have a fragrant pet.

Sprinkle dried lavender, tansy and pennyroyal around pet beds and under furniture, as fleas hate the fragrances of these herbs. An amethyst crystal in pet water is also said to deter fleas (see page 151).

To deter flies from animal food dishes, place dried sprigs or pots of eau de cologne mint and basil nearby.

Appendix 3
Flower remedies for pets

Although flower remedies are not medicinal as such, they seem to work more immediately on animals than humans; perhaps this is because animals are so receptive to healing on a spiritual level. I have suggested Bach remedies since these are probably the most widely obtainable worldwide and were the original remedies to be created.

Dr Edward Bach (1886–1936) was a British medical consultant, homeopath and bacteriologist who developed a natural medicine based on plant and flower essences. The remedies I have listed seem especially helpful for animals and birds, although they were not specifically created for them. However, there are numerous varieties of flower and tree essences made all over the world, and in Useful Reading I have suggested a book in which you can read about the different varieties. I have also listed suppliers, including the Australian essences that are available by mail order worldwide and are specifically designed for pets (see Resources). The following are some of Dr Bach's remedies:

Agrimony
Very good for dogs that act as guides or assistants, horses, or animals in the rescue services, where they may become exhausted or stressed, but show no outward signs. Agrimony is also helpful for any creatures with skin irritations and those out of their natural habitat that find it hard to settle.

Aspen

This essence calms very highly strung creatures of all kinds and pets during storms. It also relieves pets that are anxious in new surroundings; for example, after a house move. Also useful for animals and birds that find it hard to rest or sleep.

Beech

Effective for irritable, snappy creatures that are unreliable with children and other animals, especially young ones; beech is also good for horses that are unfriendly to new or novice riders. Use it to cure the constant yappers, yowlers and screechers of the animal and bird kingdom. Beech also relieves food faddiness.

Centaury

Give centaury to a creature that is easily bullied by others, and for all creatures that spend time confined; for example, a bird in a cage or a horse that is stabled for long periods. Centaury prevents creatures becoming over-sensitive to owners' moods, and is also helpful for a mother animal during a long labour or long illness, and if a pet seems to lose the will to fight.

Cerato

Effective for all animals that need to be trained, whether for obedience, for show purposes, birds of prey in controlled flight or those that work to assist humans. Cerato helps an animal to remain loyal to its owner(s), and, if sprinkled around entrances, prevents a creature straying or becoming lost. It is also good for cats that do not have well-developed homing instincts.

Cherry plum

Another excellent remedy for highly strung or temperamental creatures, notably horses that bite or kick, or may panic in traffic. Cherry plum minimises destructive behaviour with indoor creatures, such as chewing, feather plucking or scratching furniture, and reduces sensitivity to loud noises or traffic. Give cherry plum to male animals when breeding to stop aggressive behaviour, and females on heat to prevent them rejecting a mate.

Chestnut bud
An essence for retraining if bad habits develop, chestnut bud teaches animals physical boundaries; for example, dogs to return when called when off the leash. It is also useful for establishing emotional boundaries, such as not attacking other animals or jumping up at people. It may make a large, clumsy dog more aware of obstacles, especially in a confined space.

Chicory
Soothing for over-possessive animals that constantly demand attention, and reduces jealousy of other family members. Chicory also helps when an animal insists on sleeping with owners and for constant barking, yowling or screeching if owners go out.

Crab apple
Useful for animals that become obsessive about food or cleaning themselves, crab apple is also helpful for removing the pollutants and noise that can adversely affect creatures in the modern world. It is also excellent for rescue animals to help them relax.

Holly
Useful for reducing jealousy or resentment of new family members whether another animal, a baby or partner; holly also makes irritable, aggressive creatures more tolerant of others.

Honeysuckle
This essence is very helpful for a creature that has lost its mate or if a family member has gone away permanently or died. Sprinkle honeysuckle essence – diluted in water – around the bed of a young animal newly separated from its mother and siblings.

Impatiens

Another good remedy for creatures that become easily irritated by other animals, impatiens is also effective for reducing confrontations in aviaries or in shared small animal enclosures. It also makes an animal more receptive to training, especially in communal obedience classes. Impatiens is excellent for assistance animals if they show signs of overwork.

Mimulus

The essence, mimulus, overcomes fear of specific noises or places. It is helpful for a small animal that has been roughly handled by children or a previous owner, and is good for horses who are easily startled.

Oak

An excellent remedy to induce patience in a creature that is temporarily immobilised because of an illness or injury, oak helps large animals, especially horses, to pace themselves. It also strengthens helper animals.

Olive

Use olive to aid recovery in an animal worn out by a long illness or treatment, or one that accidentally strayed and has had to fend for itself. It is also useful for animals that have lost a mate or suffered a family break-up or loss.

Rock rose

The essence for all very small or timid creatures, rock rose will help accustom them to being handled by humans. It is soothing for any highly strung creature or when an animal or bird has been frightened or hurt.

Star of Bethlehem

This is a very reassuring essence if sprayed round the home during the 48 hours before you must leave a pet, whether to go away on business or holiday. Use star of Bethlehem also before an animal or bird needs to stay overnight at the vet. It is also helpful for house moves.

Sweet chestnut

Effective if a pet becomes withdrawn or depressed, sweet chestnut also restores lost appetite and enthusiasm. It is excellent for any formerly abused or neglected animals you take in to help allow trust to regrow.

Vervain

As a herb, vervain can be too strong for some creatures. As an essence, however, it soothes hyperactive and restless animals, especially those subject to a great deal of stress, perhaps because of quarrels in the human family or a major upheaval. Vervain also slows down pets that are constantly jumping and demanding human attention.

Walnut

Sometimes called the remedy of change, walnut is useful for animals and birds as well as humans. It assists an acceptance of change in the environment or the people around the creature. It is also good for retraining and breaking bad habits; for example, it may be worth trying if a bird is constantly plucking out its feathers.

Appendix 4
Pet names

Admiral (m): after the high-ranking naval officer. Suitable for pets that are autocratic and bossy, but protective of owners from when they are young. It is applicable to horses and parrots alike.

Alexander (m): the man who defends, after the famous Macedonian general Alexander the Great, who conquered much of the known world. Good for large, noble animals.

Alexandra (f): popular in Russia and Eastern Europe, equally regal for thoroughbred horses and pedigree dogs and cats. For less aristocratic creatures the diminutive **Sandy (m or f)** refers to the colour and the animal usually has an equable disposition; also the Russian female form **Sasha**.

Ambassador (m): a natural peacemaker and a creature slow to anger but with great endurance; good especially for larger creatures, such as horses.

Amber (f): originally Arabic, named after the orange organic gem made of fossilised tree resin, said to contain the souls of many tigers; used for all kinds of animals with a golden/orange tint and lively disposition. Popular especially for cats and guinea pigs.

Angel (m and f): means 'a messenger' in ancient Greek language. Originally used for gentle, female, delicate creatures of all kinds, from birds to fish to tiny dogs. The male Spanish form is now back in fashion worldwide after the cult series *Angel*, which featured a reformed vampire dedicated to doing good.

Argos (m): name of Odysseus's faithful dog who, in Homer's *Odyssey*, waited for his master to return from the Trojan wars; when Odysseus returned in disguise after many years journeying, the dog was the only one to recognise him, but his heart burst with joy and he died. It is an excellent name for an assistance dog or any loyal hound.

Ariel (m/f): Hebrew for 'lion of God', popular because of the name of the spirit of air in Shakespeare's *Tempest*, given especially to birds or swift horses.

Arion (m): Greek, means 'warlike'. According to the myth, Arion was a horse created by the sea god Poseidon; its right feet were those of a man, it had a human voice and ran as swift as the wind. Suitable for any very intelligent horse.

Aslan (m): hero saviour lion from C. S. Lewis's Narnia stories; used for large leonine dogs, assistance animals or horses with shaggy manes.

Babushka (f): Russian for old woman/grandmother. She was famed in a myth for being too busy to travel with the Three Wise Men to Bethlehem. It is a popular name with fluffy creatures, such as rabbits, any breeding animal or motherly creatures obtained later in their life.

Bandito (m): Spanish for 'an ingenious robber'. Suitable for birds, especially for parrots and animals that are charismatic but devious.

Barney (m): diminutive of Barnabas, Aramaic for 'son of consolation'. Ideal for any cheerful creature, large or small, fur or feathered.

Benita (f)/Benito (m): Spanish from the Latin Benedictus, meaning 'blessed'. Used for all kinds of creatures, especially those that come from a rescue centre.

Blue (m): a popular name for animals with a blue-grey coat. Through the tales of the American West, it has become a name for faithful creatures, especially horses and dogs.

Bob/Bobbie (m/f): French/German diminutive of Robert, meaning 'of great fame/brightness'; used for cheerful, willing dogs, especially those of indeterminate parentage, also for patient horses.

Boot/s (m): any creature with distinctive leg or paw markings that resemble boots. Popularised in a UK 1950s comic strip as a scruffy Old English sheepdog, which has retained a cult following in the UK.

Bran (m): Celtic name of the protector god, meaning 'raven', who is said to guard England from invasion. A popular bird name, especially for large dark-coloured ones and also for strongly built horses.

Bucephalus (m): wild horse tamed by Alexander the Great as a young boy who rode him in battle and, after his death, built the city of Bucephala, as a memorial to his beloved horse. It is an excellent name for a wild but loving stallion.

Buffy (f): originally used to refer to the yellowy cream colour, but since the popularity of the cult TV series *Buffy the Vampire Slayer*, now chosen for feisty female creatures, especially rabbits or more exotic pets.

Caer (f): Celtic name; she was the fairy maiden of Connacht in Ireland who assumed the form of a swan that sang with great beauty. Use for any bird or graceful creature.

Caleb (m): Hebrew name meaning dog; Caleb was one of the few Israelites who, after the Exodus with Moses, reached the Promised Land. Use for a devoted canine or horse.

Casey (m): a Celtic name, meaning in Ireland 'courageous' or 'ever-watchful'. It was made popular in the US by Casey Jones, a nineteenth-century engine driver who saved his passengers by sacrificing his own life. Use for reckless, buccaneering but devoted birds and animals.

Cass/Cassandra/Cassie (f): the Greek name means 'shining on mankind'; she was a Trojan prophetess who was cursed by Apollo to speak the truth but never to be believed. It is popular with willowy dogs, mysterious cats and inscrutable horses.

Charlie (m): German diminutive of Charles, which means 'free man', and a popular name for kings and emperors everywhere. **Charles** is good for large aristocratic animals; the more popular Charlie, immortalised in Steinbeck's book of his travels with his dog Charlie, is given to cheerful companions whether fur or feathered.

Chester (m): an old English form of the Roman '*castra*', legion or fortified camp, originally a place name in north-west England. It is good for horses or quirky birds and animals.

Cinders/Cindy (f): for grey-coloured animals, especially those found or rescued, named after the fairytale character Cinderella (from the French '*cendre*' – ashes). It is also short for Lucinda, from the Latin for 'light'. It is a good name, therefore, for birds or animals that are comforting, always outgoing and optimistic.

Circe (f): Greek enchantress whose name, Kirkos, means 'falcon', who was daughter of the Greek sun god, Helios, and the sea nymph, Perse. According to the Roman writer Pliny, Circe commanded all the stars that controlled humankind's fate; her name is often given to exotic pet birds, birds of prey or creatures from other lands, as well as pet pigs, because of her fondness for turning sailors into swine.

Cleo (f): diminutive of Cleopatra, the ancient Egyptian queen, last of the Ptolemies; a name used especially for cats and all creatures of grace and beauty, including fish.

Darwin (m): from an Old English word meaning 'beloved friend'; made famous by Charles Darwin who put forward the theory of evolution and by the Australian city named after him. It is excellent for all curious animals and birds of any size.

Denver (m): 'safe valley' in Anglo-Saxon and popularised by the town in Colorado. Denvers always find food within ten seconds of entering their new home. Good for natural entrepreneurs in any species.

Dexter (m): from the Latin for 'on the right, the favoured direction'; a name for happy-go-lucky creatures of all kinds.

Dinah/Dina (f): Hebrew for 'judgement'; a popular name with dogs and rabbits, but can be used for any reliable creatures that show no inclination of straying from the fireside on being brought home.

Dixie (f): derived from the French '*dix*' which means 'ten'; used especially in the American South where *dix* was printed on some dollar bills and associated with jazz musicians. A name for lively and vocal animals and birds of all kinds.

Dolly (f): diminutive of Dorothea, Greek for 'gift of god'; a name for all gentle creatures from horses to rabbits and doves. Popular with pet sheep after Dolly of cloning fame.

Duke (m): more American West than aristocratic English where it originated as a high title for a noble; also a popular form of Marmaduke. Used for large, reliable animals.

Dusty (m or f): from Dustin, a Viking name meaning 'Thor, the thunder god's stone'; often used for brown, homely dogs, especially with more heart than pedigree.

Epona (f): the Celtic Romano horse goddess who is still commemorated in white horses on chalk hills in England; used for all noble steeds and especially brood mares, as Epona was a symbol of fertility.

Ermintrude (f): a German name meaning 'dearly beloved'; a straightforward routine-loving pet, often used for pet ducks or geese, rabbits or cats; also for pet calves.

Esmeralda (f): Spanish for the precious, green gem emerald; popular with pet goats, ducks, rabbits and cats that walk alone.

Felix (m): from the Latin for 'lucky' or 'fortunate', especially used for cats that seem to be accident-prone and have nine lives.

Ferdinand (m): from the German meaning 'peace' or 'ready to journey'; a regal name used for show bulls, but also all kinds of creatures including birds that are keen to explore but always return home.

Freyja (f): a Viking name of the goddess of love and beauty; often given to black cats because, according to myth, Freyja's chariot was pulled by two large black cats. Also used for any beautiful long-haired or plumed creature.

Gabriel (m): from the Hebrew meaning 'man of God'; the archangel of the Moon and one of the main messenger archangels; suitable for any creature, such as carrier pigeons, animals that are very energetic, goats and for those that are traditionally nocturnal.

Ginger (m/f): a hot, yellow-red-coloured spice, hence used for red-coated creatures of all kinds, especially those that are bursting with life; also diminutive of Virginia. From the Latin for 'a maiden' and the US state.

Goldie (f): derived from the word 'gold'; used for all creatures including fish that are golden in colour. Goldie tends to be a name that indicates loyalty and devotion in the pet, i.e. 'heart of gold'.

Hero (m): derived from Greek *heros* for bravery, originally a female name in ancient Greece. Most pets with this name live up to it and will be plucky and resourceful in the care of their owners (see page 92).

Holly (m/f): Old English for the prickly evergreen shrub; in the myth, 'King of the Dark half of the year'; popular for animals with spiky coats or those bought or obtained around Christmas.

Homer (m): originally an ancient Greek name meaning 'pledge', given to the writer of the epics *Iliad* and *Odyssey*;

also given light-hearted connotations by the cult cartoon character Homer Simpson. The name is used especially for horses and dogs that are very distractible, a garrulous bird or, in the traditional sense, for a very dignified creature.

Honey (f): from Old English 'honeg'; used especially for honey-coloured Labradors, but also any sweet-natured animal, large or tiny.

Horus (m): the ancient Egyptian falcon-headed sky god; used for all birds, not only those that are predators.

Jarapiri (m): the creator snake in Australian Aboriginal myth that made the landscape and the waterholes; good for any reptile or lizard.

Jemima (f): from the Hebrew 'dove' and therefore a popular name for birds, pet ducks and geese; also after Beatrix Potter's Jemima Puddleduck. The name is also good for pet goats and sheep and fastidious cats.

Jenny (f): a Welsh name and a form of King Arthur's wife's name, Guinevere. Although it means 'white', it is nevertheless used for all kinds of gentle animals and birds.

Jess (f): diminutive of Hebrew, means 'gift'. The name is used for all loyal animals, especially popular for cats and horses.

Lady (f): for any aristocratic animal, since Disney's *Lady and the Tramp*, especially pedigree bitches of a docile nature.

Lucky (m): popular name, like Felix; tends to be used for pets with an easy-going, take-life-as-it-comes attitude.

Macavity (m): the mystery cat of T. S. Eliot's poems and latterly the musical *Cats* fame. Known in the poem as 'the hidden paw', Macavity is definitely a good name for a wanderer or a cat that seems to have secrets.

Marmaduke (m): Irish name for follower of St Maedoc; suitable for almost any pet, from horses to gerbils, that displays instant attachment and devotion to a new owner(s).

Marquis/Marquise (m): Old French for 'ruler of the border lands'; good for noble horses and large dogs; also for parrots and any creature acquired later in its life.

Max (m): diminutive of **Maximilian**, 'he who is the greatest of all'; an imperial name, therefore suitable for horses in its full form or as Max for an adventurous dog or gossipy bird.

Merlin (m): a Welsh name meaning 'fortress of the sea'; magician of King Arthur who often took the form of a hawk; therefore associated with pets that are intuitive from when young, for beautiful horses or for birds.

Mickey (m): diminutive of **Michael**, a Hebrew name meaning 'is like the Lord'; the full archangel name is wonderful for creatures of a fiery nature or horses with flowing manes. Mickey suits cheerful animals and, especially since the Disney character Mickey Mouse, all rodent pets.

Missy (f): diminutive of Latin Melissa that means 'honey bee' and therefore is usually given to small, sweet-natured animals and birds.

Misty (f): an Old English name meaning 'shrouded in mist', good for all grey animals, but especially small, shy ones, such as guinea pigs.

Molly/Mally (f): the Irish diminutive for Mary; popular with country animals, especially big dogs, donkeys, pet sheep, calves and pigs.

Ossian/Oisin (m): Celtic hero name from Irish legend, meaning 'little deer', because his mother, **Saba**, was enchanted into the form of a deer and raised the golden-haired boy in a cave in her deer form. Use this or his mother's name for any shy, quiet, loving animals that display flashes of courage and determination.

Otto (m): German diminutive for 'wealthy'; associated with royalty. It is good for all show animals or regal, pedigree creatures of any size; also for intelligent horses.

Pegasus (m): the winged flying horse of Minerva, goddess of wisdom in Graeco-Roman legend; the horse was given to the young warrior Bellerophon, to overcome the dragon-like monster Chimaera. A good name for swift stallions and show horses, also for feisty donkeys and birds.

Pepper (m): a spice. A name given to creatures of all sizes that are very lively; popular with small wire-haired dogs.

Phoenix (m): ancient Greek/Latin name for 'dark red'; mythical golden bird that lived for 500 years, then consumed itself on a funeral pyre, before rising golden and renewed from the ashes. The name is suitable not only for birds, but also for all beautiful golden-coloured creatures.

Prince (m): another regal name from the Latin, this time from *princeps*, meaning 'the chief or leader'; given to large animals, such as horses or dogs that are fiercely protective.

Roosevelt (m): a Dutch word for 'field of roses', made famous by two US presidents; suitable for any creature that shows initiative and a unique personal character from an early age. It is a good name also for show animals of all kinds.

Roswell (m): Anglo-Saxon for 'horse stream'; given new meaning by the alien space landing at Roswell in the US; a good name for horses or any unusual, quirky pet.

Rufus (m): Latin for 'red'; made famous by the Norman king William Rufus, who was killed by an arrow in the back while out hunting. It is used for red-coated dogs, also chestnut horses and any small, plucky creatures.

Sally/Sallie (f): diminutive of Sarah, Hebrew for princess; suitable for any affectionate, docile creature.

Sam (m/f): diminutive of the Hebrew Samuel, the listener of God; feminine form **Samantha**, for patient, quiet companions, fur or feathered, gentle donkeys and miniature horses.

Samson (m): Hebrew for the Sun. The biblical Samson was famed for his immense strength and his long hair, until it was cut (leading to his downfall); popular with all large, long-haired animals, or, in contrast, tiny feisty creatures or garrulous birds.

Sekhmet (f): the ancient Egyptian fierce lion-headed goddess who was also a healer and protectress; for independent but protective cats and dogs and guide dogs of all kinds, long-maned horses, reptiles and all exotic pets.

Shadow (m): not only for grey-black pets of all kinds, from horses to koi carp, but also ones with a hidden side to their nature or who hide.

Shane (m/f): from Ireland; diminutive of Celtic Sean (John) which means in Hebrew 'God is gracious'; popular with dogs and horses, especially outgoing ones, but can be used for any creature that is faithful, and, with its American West connotations, for any creature that goes the extra mile.

Silvester/Sylvester (f): Latin name meaning 'dweller in the forest'; popularised by Sylvester Stallone (and made more adventurous and macho). Popular also with cartoon creatures. The name is often given to animals that are natural clowns, from rodents to parrots to dogs and horses, the last two displaying the more macho aspects.

Susie/Suzy (f): diminutive of Susanna, Hebrew for 'lily'; often given to cuddly pets with a docile nature.

Tabitha (f): New Testament name from the Hebrew meaning 'doe' or 'gazelle'; used for tabby cats with a homely nature; also for house rabbits, pet mice and gerbils.

Tess/Tessie (f): diminutive of Theresa, a name from the Mediterranean region, originating from the Greek island Thera; especially favoured for gentle dogs, but suitable for other affectionate animals and slow-moving horses or donkeys.

Tiger/Tigger (m): Tigger was named after A. A. Milne's inept tiger and so the name is generally for hyperactive creatures that are often in trouble through no fault of their own. Also for stripy or marmalade cats, and it is a popular name for hamsters with a stripe, too.

Toby (m): diminutive of Tobias, the Greek form, a hero who defeated demons with the assistance of the archangel Raphael; the Hebrew name Tobiah means 'God is good'. Often given to patient, reliable, affectionate creatures, from horses to rabbits and guinea pigs.

Valmai (f): Australian name meaning 'mayflower'; good for animals obtained in the month of May or for birds, as another meaning is 'May falcon'.

Valentine (m): from the Latin for 'strong and healthy'; popularised by the saint of love; therefore given to animals and birds obtained around 14 February or that are destined to break human and animal hearts with their liquid eyes and charismatic ways.

Wolf/Wolfgang (m): German from the word for 'wolf' or 'tracks of the wolf'; used for large dogs or those used for guard or assistance work; also for horses.

Wilma (f): Germanic form of Wilhelmina from Wilhelm, meaning 'protection'; given to willing, eager-to-please creatures of all kinds, especially those that are protective even when tiny.

Appendix 5
Animal strengths
and qualities

In Chapters 10 and 11 I described how you can use animals and birds as symbols to give you strength, power or protection when you need it. By choosing animals and birds not only from the list that follows but also those you encounter either in real life, on video or in photographs, you can absorb their relevant good qualities to give you what you need; for example, courage or adaptability. This symbolic psychological process is a good way of getting in touch with and increasing the same powers that already exist within you.

Some of the creatures I have listed here are mythical – these are just some that I have worked with successfully both personally and when teaching. You can easily create your own list or make additions to mine.

Bat
Learning to trust your intuitive radar, overcoming hidden fears, especially of the dark, acknowledging and transforming the less positive aspects of your personality.

Bear
Protectiveness, strength and endurance, fierceness to repel foes – especially those threatening its kin – wisdom that comes from the experience of life.

Beaver
Adaptability, home-making wherever it finds itself, perseverance, harmony with the world in which it lives.

Blackbird
Joy bringer; the ability to cast away fear, no matter how overwhelming the odds against you; defence of territory, cheerfulness in adversity.

Boar (wild)
Tenacity, courage, ability to outface threats and delight in sensual pleasure.

Buffalo (bison)
Generosity of spirit, bringer of abundance, optimism for better times ahead, spiritual focus.

Bull
Strength, power to win through, survival instincts, increased potency/productivity in all aspects of life.

Butterfly
Transformation and renewal of life; ability to enjoy every moment of happiness; power to live in the present without fretting over past or future.

Cat
Spiritual powers, intuition, ability to relate instantly to worldly demands without becoming engulfed by them.

Chameleon
Keeping a low profile when necessary, sensitivity to atmospheres, moods and the environment.

Cougar/mountain lion
Stealth, focus, ability to seize an opportunity; a creature that can hunt alone, without needing others for strength.

Crane
Learning from personal past experiences, acquiring wisdom, ability to keep one's counsel, bringer of health and long life.

Crocodile

Protection against physical dangers and mental aggressiveness; for sharp thinking and the will to go after what you really want, and the patience to wait for the right moment.

Crow/jackdaw

Initiating change, to regain parts of yourself you have buried or lost, to find spiritual treasure or advantage in unexpected places and to weather hard times.

Deer

Swiftness of response, grace and gentleness, sensitivity to the emotions of others.

Dingo/wild dogs

Fierce defence of own kin, making own destiny; fearlessness and tenacity.

Dolphin

Empathy with others, intuitive power, healing abilities and acute intelligence.

Dove

Inner peace and peacemaking abilities; power to anticipate the needs and feelings of others; for learning to trust or trust again.

Dragon

Creative power, bringing out hidden potential in self, revealing potency in a crisis or challenge, catalyst for change.

Eagle

Soaring vision, unlimited potential idealism and nobility of spirit, leadership.

Frog

Bringing fertility and abundance in every way into your life, ability to move naturally from one stage of life and relationships to the next, renewal of hope and opportunity after a stagnant or difficult period.

Goose/duck

To incubate new beginnings, to launch ideas into the real world, and to flow with your own wise feelings that may be the best guide to action.

Gull

Expressing your true nature; seeking more personal autonomy, following your heart and not your head where personal happiness is concerned.

Hawk/falcon/kestrel

To focus on what you really need, expanding horizons both mentally and spiritually, gaining a sense of perspective about life and taking decisive action when needed.

Heron

For bringing freedom into your own life and those around you, for developing optimism for each new day and leaving behind what is redundant in your life.

Horse

Harmony with others, fertility, stamina, controlled power and the enthusiasm for new places, people and ideas.

Hound/dog

Boundless energy and enthusiasm, attracting loyalty in others, remaining true to yourself, for casting a protective boundary around yourself and those you love.

Jaguar/leopard

To protect yourself if you travel or work at night, for courage and for hunting new opportunities.

Lion

For courage, wise authority and for developing mature

wisdom whatever your age; also vigilance in making sure you are not deceived.

Monkey
Curiosity about life and people, inventiveness, ingenuity in problem solving, dexterity of thought, being aware of place in family/social/work networks.

Opossum
Ability to adapt to and survive in less than ideal circumstances, to avoid confrontation if the odds are against you and to follow convention or the majority until you can live your own way.

Otter
Balancing different demands on time and priorities, offering service to others, ability to overcome difficulties with cheerfulness and, if necessary, by uprooting.

Owl
Learning to listen to your inner voice, to keep one's own counsel, for acquiring wisdom and to seize the moment swiftly and silently rather than constantly rehearsing strategies.

Parrot
Increased communication, sociability, ability to understand and adapt to others' lifestyles and environments.

Peacock
Allowing others to see your talents and hard work; expressing your inner creativity, bringing natural beauty and colour wherever you can into your world.

Pelican
Care of the young or the vulnerable, unselfishness, ability to use available resources creatively and value what you have, rather than wishing for what you have not.

Phoenix
Regeneration after loss or difficulty, striving for perfection, maintaining health and harmony in a stressful world.

Rabbit
Sensitivity to subtle signals in environment and from others, intense fertility and productivity, ability to mentally outrun predators and avoid confrontations you cannot win.

Ram
For meeting challenges head on, for acknowledging your own creative sexuality, and release of unnecessary inhibitions, perhaps left over from the past.

Salmon
Appreciation of home and family roots, evolved intuitive powers; recalling wisdom, especially from inherited family wisdom.

Snake
Ability to shed what is no longer of value in life, female wisdom and alertness to potential hazards, especially protection against spite and human venom.

Squirrel
Conservation of resources, working with rather than ignoring or fighting natural energy levels, proficient in keeping part of ability and power in reserve.

Stag
Invincibility, willingness to fight for beliefs, pride in personal strength and talents.

Swan
Inner stillness, grace, transformation of life, increasing creativity.

Tiger
Courage, commitment to pursuit of desires and needs, passion for life, ability to conceal fierceness until the right time.

Unicorn
Valuing individuality, purity of purpose in thought as well as actions, healing powers.

Wallaby
Protectiveness towards the young and vulnerable, an adventurer who is still a clan creature at heart; optimism.

Wolf
To develop your own survival instincts, fierce protectiveness of kin, home and friends, sense of connection with others, altruism.

Resources

I have listed only a representative sample of addresses that I have personally encountered, but there are many similar organisations that can be found in local telephone directories, at advice bureaux, in veterinary surgeries or on the Internet. I have given e-mail addresses or websites where I have found them.

Assistance dogs

Australia
Assistance Dogs Australia
PO Box 455, Engadine, NSW 2233
Tel: 0061 9548 3355
E-mail: abiggs@assistancedogs.org.au

UK
Canine Partners for Independence
Unit E2, The Brickyards, Steep Marsh,
Petersfield, Hants, GU32 2BN
Tel: 00 44 1730 894830
Website: www.cpiuk.org

US
American Dog Trainers Network
Website for all of US www.inch.com/dogs/service/html

Examples of state organisations:

Companion Animals of Arizona
PO Box 5006, Scottsdale, AZ 85261-5006
Tel: 001 602 258 3306

California Assistance Dogs Institute
PO Box 2234, Rohnert Park, CA 94927
Tel: 001 707 585 0300

Canine Companions for Independence
The Northeast Training Center,
PO Box 205, Farmingdale, NY 11735–0205
Tel: 001 516 694 6938

Flower remedies for animals

Australia
Marlene Keel
International Flower Essence Centre
Pet Essences, PO Box 1144
Hartwell, VIC 3124
Tel: 0061 9889 7176
E-mail: marlene@ifec.com.au
Website: www.ifec.com.au

US
Jessica Bear, ND
Balancing Essentials
348 Deauville St., Las Vegas, NV 89106
Tel: 001 702 598-0727

Flower remedies, general

Australia
Australian Native Tree Essences
The Sabian Centre
PO Box 527
Kew, Victoria, 31031
Tel: 0061 9818 1968
E-mail: sabian@netspace.net.au

UK
Bach Flower Remedies
Healing Herbs Ltd
PO Box 65, Hereford, HR2 0UW
Tel: 00 44 1873 890 218
E-mail: pc58@dial.pipex.com

Findhorn Foundation
The Park, Findhorn, Forres, IV36 0TZ
Tel: 00 44 1309 691620
E-mail: Stewards@findhorn.org

US
Nelson Bach USA Ltd
100 Research Drive
Wilmington, MA 01887

Dolphin energies

Japan
Ki and Dolphin Energy House
Genkikai, Ishizaki Kokyo and Konoe,
Daihonzan Myorenzi Gyokuryu-in,
871 Myorenzi-mae-cho, Oimyahigashi-iru,
Teranouchi-dori Kamigyo-ku, Kyoto
Tel: 0081 451 0058

US
Lynn Phillips
The Dolphin Circle
Tel: 001 425 334-0272
E-mail: iamdavid@premier1.net

CDs for swimming with dolphins at home

US
Dolphin Love CD,
World Disc Productions
PO Box 2749, Friday Harbor, WA 98250

Protecting wildlife

Australia
World Wildlife Fund
Level 5, 725 George Street, NSW 2001
Tel: 0061 9281 5515
E-mail: enquiries@wwf.org.au

New Zealand
World Wildlife Fund
The Treehouse, Botanic Gardens,
Glenmae St, Wellington
Tel: 0064 4992 930
E-mail: info@wwf.org.nz

UK
World Wildlife Fund
Panda House, Weyside Park,
Godalming, Surrey, GU7 1XR
Tel: 00 44 1463 426444

US
World Wildlife Fund
1250-24th Street NW, Washington DC, 20037 1175
Tel: 001 202 293 4800

Rescue organizations

UK
Bev Doyle Home Rescue
17 Hayle Road
Oldham OL1 4NR
E-mail: bev@homerescue.net

Useful reading

Some of the books listed are quite old, but in my opinion are worth reading. A number of these are still in print but you may also come across others in old bookshops or for sale privately on the Internet.

Animal books
Ted Andrews, *Animal Speak*, Llewellyn, 2002
V. Briton, *Alternative Therapies for Horses: A New Approach to Health and Fitness*, Sterling Publishing Co., 1995
Beryl Chapman, *Homeopathic Treatment of Birds*, C. W. Daniel Co. Ltd, 1991
D. Fossey, *Gorillas in the Mist*, Houghton-Mifflin, 1985
Martin Goldstein, *The Nature of Animal Healing*, Ballantine Books, 2000
Pat Lazarus, *Keep Your Pet Healthy the Natural Way*, Keats Publishing Inc., 1983
Corrine Miller Kenner, *Psychic Pets and Spirit Animals*, Llewellyn, 1996
M. Raymonde-Hawkins and G. Macleod, *The Raystede Handbook of Homoeopathic Remedies for Animals*, C. W. Daniel Co. Ltd, 1985
Diane Stein, *Natural Healing for Cats and Dogs*, Crossing Press, 1996
John Sutton, *Psychic Pets*, Bloomsbury, 1997
Lisa Tenzin Dolma, *Swimming with Dolphins: A Healing Experience*, Foulsham, 1997

Auras and general healing
Barbara Anne Brennan, *Hands of Light*, Bantam Books, 1987
Cassandra Eason, *Aura Reading*, Piatkus, 2000

Crystals and crystal healing
Cassandra Eason, *Crystal Healing*, Quantum, 2001
Phyllis Galde, *Crystal Healing: The Next Step*, Llewellyn Books, 1991

Flower remedies
Claire Harvey and Amanda Cochrane, *The Encyclopaedia of Flower Remedies*, Thorsons/Harper Collins, 1995

Index